THE BACK

28^{95}

Series Titles

Squatter
Yolanda DeLoach

Soul of the Outdoors
Dave Greschner

The Arc of the Escarpment
Robert Root

We Come from Good Stock
Kay Oakes Oring

Wildlifer
Neil F. Payne

From the Heart: The Story of Matrix
John Harmon

The Long Fields
Anne-Marie Oomen

Kick Out the Bottom
Erik Mortenson & Christopher Kramer

Wrong Tree: Adventures in Wildlife Biology
Jeff Wilson

At the Lake
Jim Landwehr

Body Talk
Takwa Gordon

The In-Between State
Martha Lundin

North Freedom
Carolyn Dallmann

Ohio Apertures
Robert Miltner

Praise for

Squatter

"A courageous story. Yolanda's vivid descriptions of the Ice Age Trail's beauty, obstacles and emancipation, brought back wonderful memories of my own hike. Yolanda also weaves a challenging emotional journey into the narrative with a raw honesty that entices the reader. Successful memoir writing is not about what you did, it's about what you did with it."

—Ed Abell
author of *My Father's Keep*

"*Squatter* takes us along on the hike of Yolanda DeLoach's life as she faces demons and then meets angels. She shows us what trail magic is all about. A book for readers wanting proof of the healing powers of nature to be discovered within themselves and along the Ice Age Trail."

—Patty Dreier
Past President of the Ice Age Trail Alliance
author of *Empowered: One Planet at a Time*

"Many people use long-distance hiking–whether intentionally or subconsciously–as a way to heal. That includes Yolanda DeLoach, whose memoir about her trek along the Ice Age Trail beautifully showcases both the wonders of this National Scenic Trail and how therapeutic hiking can be."

—Melanie Radzicki McManus
author of *Thousand-Miler: Adventures Hiking the Ice Age Trail*

SQUATTER

ONE WOMAN'S JOURNEY TO RECLAIM HER SPIRIT ON THE ICE AGE TRAIL

Yolanda DeLoach

CORNERSTONE PRESS
UNIVERSITY OF WISCONSIN-STEVENS POINT

Cornerstone Press, Stevens Point, Wisconsin 54481
Copyright © 2024 Yolanda DeLoach
www.uwsp.edu/cornerstone

Printed in the United States of America by
Point Print and Design Studio, Stevens Point, Wisconsin

Library of Congress Control Number: 2023950460
ISBN: 978-1-960329-33-2

Photographs by Yolanda DeLoach

All rights reserved.

This book is a memoir. Some names have been changed and court records sealed to protect privacy. The events depicted in this story are a reflection of the author's experiences and may not be how others recall the events. The author in no way represents any company, corporation, or brand, mentioned herein. The views expressed in this memoir are solely those of the author.

Cornerstone Press titles are produced in courses and internships offered by the Department of English at the University of Wisconsin–Stevens Point.

DIRECTOR & PUBLISHER
Dr. Ross K. Tangedal

EXECUTIVE EDITORS
Jeff Snowbarger, Freesia McKee

EDITORIAL DIRECTOR
Ellie Atkinson

SENIOR EDITORS
Brett Hill, Grace Dahl

PRESS STAFF
Chloe Ciezynski, Carolyn Czerwinski, Alex Diaz, Kenzie Kierstyn, Sophie McPherson, Maddy Mauthe, Kylie Newton, Josh Paulson, Natalie Reiter, Katie Schimke, Ava Willett

*For anyone who knows they need to leave a destructive relationship but can't find the way out.
I see you.*

Ice Age National Scenic Trail

The Ice Age Trail was approximately 1,147 miles from spring of 2020 to spring of 2021. The trail is always changing as new segments are added and expanded.

For more information check out iceagetrail.org.

Part One

I'm emotionally not in a good place. I've let Mitch back into my life because I can't let go. I know he's not good for me. I know that. But he's so persistent, I don't know how to end it. He'll always be here. He'll always show up. The scary thing is, part of me wants him to, and I don't know why.

1

I want you to feel safe with me.
—Mitch, November 2017

People liked Mitch when they first met him. His wit, smile, and gentle nature drew people in. While playing pool at a dive bar once, a man came up to him and asked, "Hey! Are you dat guy on TV?" Mitch wasn't on TV, but he gave off the I'm-a-guy-on-TV vibes. At 6'3 with a mass of curly hair that could be tamed for a sharp, professional look, he attracted attention.

Even animals liked Mitch. He showed me a video of a mama duck leading her babies right past his feet while he sat by a lake. I thought animals sensed goodness in people, as if they had a direct view into a person's heart. A protective mama duck surely wouldn't lead her babies to the feet of a dark soul. After a bird flew into his living room window, he kept it in a box while it recovered. I thought he was a hero for doing that.

I met Mitch online, and we arranged a stereotypical coffee first date for the morning of November 4, 2017. The season's first snow had fallen during the night. I raised the blinds to reveal my backyard blanketed in white, and whispered, "I'm going to meet someone special today." I had never been on a real, respectable date before. And I was a widowed forty-nine-year-old with two grandchildren. During my youth, meeting guys mostly involved drinking and sex.

I didn't have many of the social experiences that others took for granted. Instead of going off to college, or the military, I got married at the age of eighteen. After seeing my scores for testing that I didn't prepare for, my high school guidance counselor had said, "You'll never make it in college." So, I married my boyfriend because it was something to do. I felt there were no other options and left home unprepared for adult life. My teenage, out-of-control spiral led that first marriage to an abrupt end a year later. I walked away from it one day and into the arms of an older man who was more than willing to give a lost nineteen-year-old the attention she subconsciously craved. He taught me how to drive a semi, and I spent a year on the road with him driving a truck (this was the late 1980s, and I'm sure the CDL requirements were different than today). Weeks after turning twenty-one, I married him. Again, it was something to do. I had zero confidence in myself to pursue anything else. He was seventeen years my senior. We went on to have five kids together. The marriage lasted an unfulfilling twenty-eight years. It was a calm, stable relationship, but I didn't love him. I stayed with someone I didn't love because of my determination to do something right for once.

* * *

I walked through inches of slush across the Starbucks parking lot in Wausau, Wisconsin, wearing knee-high boots and perfectly fitted jeans. I looked pretty darn good. Inside, a slim man also wearing jeans and a green, button-down shirt, towered over everyone around him. He looked to be my age, but I knew from his dating profile, he was eleven years my senior. "Yolanda?" he asked with a shy smile that put me at ease. We ordered, and his quick wit made the barista laugh. "You're so funny," she said before making our drinks. Being with someone so likable and humorous felt good. He must be someone light and easy to get along with, I thought.

We talked for three hours that morning at Starbucks. Mitch seemed to be a good listener. He talked about his outdoor adventures. "I've been to Isle Royale National Park over forty times, mostly kayaking or canoeing, sometimes backpacking. I even had an encounter with the wolf pack there," he said, boasting a bit. But I expected a guy to do some puffing himself up on a first date. Even in nature, male birds have to dance around and show off their impressive feathers. He was nice enough. Being a practical person, I didn't believe in the fireworks of love at first sight, so the date wasn't exceptional. But it was enjoyable. I was interested in seeing him again.

After arriving home, I went to my room and cried. I imagine that's not the typical response one hopes for after a first date. It wasn't even regular crying, but bawling. I couldn't help it. The tears just flowed. The date was the first time I had done something outside the world of my home and family. It was the first time I had done something that was totally for me. I felt a bit selfish. If I pursued a new relationship, it would change my life. And my family's life. Did I really want that? Two of my five kids still lived at home. I liked my safe, predictable, comfortable bubble. Change is hard.

Our second date was the following day. As we hiked at a local state park, I mentioned petty things we sometimes do in life, trying to be transparent and real.

"Sometimes we do the dumbest things," I said. Mitch told me that years ago his now ex-wife was upset with their young son about something.

"I listened from the next room, wrote down what she said and stuck the paper in a drawer," Mitch said. He glanced at me with a coy smile.

I laughed. "Yep, that's a petty thing," I said, thinking that he shared it because he grew and learned something from doing that. I later discovered he did that all the time. He collected ammunition.

Mitch could get people to tell him their life stories. His charisma drew people out. A year into our relationship, he went to see a banker about a loan for a house we were going to buy. They sat in his office, and the banker spilled all the trouble he had with his girlfriend and her son. He poured out his soul to Mitch after just meeting him. That's the effect Mitch had on people. But the odd thing was, Mitch never reciprocated. He showed me the email he received from the banker later that day. It was an awkward mix of an apology for talking too much and a thank you for listening. Mitch had presented the email to me as proof that he was a great, trustworthy guy. "See, I help people. They trust me," he said. I imagined the banker, sitting in his office after Mitch left, stunned and embarrassed.

* * *

Mitch moved things along between us. A week after our first date, he asked if I'd be in an "exclusive relationship" with him. He was educated, professional, and adventurous. He had lived in our community for thirty years and divorced after a long-term marriage. It all sounded quite normal. I hadn't developed feelings for him yet. It had only been a week. That comes with time. The thought of dating multiple people was daunting. Too complicated. He was nice enough. Why not pick one person that seemed decent and focus on him? What could go wrong? He's a normal guy from my town looking for another chance after a long marriage. Like me. I decided to give it a go.

So I said, "Sure."

Mitch churned out poetic texts. I texted him a photo of rare Merlin falcons that once nested in a giant white pine in my backyard and had been studied by some bird organization. His text response was, *Somehow, we were both carried away by Merlin falcons to a wonderland that awaits only those with the loveliest of connections and purest of hearts.* It was downright cheesy, but I fell for it. He blew up my phone hourly with similar texts.

The outdoors was a major theme in our relationship. My outdoor experiences had been child-centered: family camping, exploring creeks and woods, and canoeing with toddlers sitting stiffly in their life jackets. I was inexperienced at Mitch's level of outdoor recreation, which I found enticing. He built himself up as a competent outdoorsman who loved Lake Superior's Isle Royale National Park, an archipelago of over four hundred islands. One of his trips to the park was for the sole purpose of hiding a canoe deep into the backcountry. He concealed it in the woods surrounding Sargent Lake, a narrow, twisted body of water deeply set within the main island. No trails led to Sargent Lake which was surrounded by dense forest that demanded good navigational skills and bushwhacking to reach. "You have a canoe hidden in a national park?" I asked. I'd never met anyone like him before.

Mitch spent days muscling that canoe through Isle Royale's rugged forest. "I want to keep a canoe at Sargent Lake to have a place that is just mine…it's a lake few humans have ever seen," he said. He stashed five-gallon buckets filled with extra camping supplies and dried food around the island, ignoring the Leave-No-Trace policy of enjoying the wild. "I'm the King of Isle Royale," he said. "I want things waiting there for me." I thought the King title was him being silly, but I would later learn he held a deep sense of entitlement.

He recalled the night he slept in one of the island's caves. "I felt connected to the ancient people who once lived there," he said, enthralling me. Once he even slept under a bridge in Michigan's Upper Peninsula the night before catching the ferry to the island. "Another time I unrolled my sleeping bag at the end of a dead-end road right out under the stars…cowboy camping," he said.

"You're like some kind of adventure god," I laughed during one of his tales. He had a dirty, rugged, daring side and a clean-cut, button-down shirt and tie side. One of his earliest messages to me was, *I want you to feel safe with me.* I thought I'd met a good match for me.

But there were things I overlooked in our first few months together. He didn't want me to get a massage from a male therapist. He asked me to change out of my t-shirt. "That's too fitted, it shows too much of your shape," he insisted. I honored his requests. And I didn't know why. He questioned why I 'liked' any of my male Facebook friends' posts. He even thought up a scenario that I must have had a past affair with someone whose photo I 'liked'. The photo was of the person's bedroom after a remodeling project. "It's totally inappropriate of you to 'like' a photo of a man's bedroom," Mitch said.

I brushed off those instances as Mitch being old-school and not getting social media. Because he was so educated, I overlooked it. He had attended a venerable university out East. I respected that and ignored my gut feelings when those behaviors popped up.

SQUATTER

* * *

Four months after meeting, we flew to Hawaii. I had never been on a big trip like that before. My late husband and I didn't travel. Partly because we couldn't afford to, partly because I was always breastfeeding a child, but also, I never pushed for it because I didn't feel close to him. Once a year, all of us would ride along in my husband's semi to Texas to visit his family. Then the kids and I would return on Amtrak while my husband went on with the next delivery. The older three are now grown and gone: two in the Twin Cities area and one in the military, stationed in California. My mom agreed to look in on Liz and Grace, the two teens at home, while I went to Hawaii.

Mitch and I spent our first night tenting on a pristine beach of Hawaii's smallest island: Kauai, the Garden Isle. We awoke after a euphoric night to swaying palm trees against a morning pink sky and the pounding surf yards away. We had the day to sightsee before Mitch's older brother, Martin, and his girlfriend, Patty, flew in. We spent the rest of the trip as guests at their timeshare. Kauai would be an unforgettable, nine-day adventure, but not for the reasons I'd hoped.

"Can you please slow down?" I asked, bracing my hand on the dash as Mitch sped along the island's windy, narrow roads. He tailgated and flipped off other drivers. I had driven with him plenty of times at home and never saw him behave that way. When we arrived at the timeshare, Mitch was not pleased with the bedroom arrangements. Since we were Martin and Patty's guests at their timeshare, it only made sense that they would get the lower-level master suite and Mitch and I would get the loft.

"I want the downstairs suite!" Mitch demanded. "We're not staying upstairs!" He stomped around until he got his way and was unsympathetic to the fact that Martin had trouble navigating stairs while recovering from cellulitis in one of his lower legs. "It's not a big deal, we'll take the loft," Martin said, caving in to Mitch's demand in a way that made me think that he was used to Mitch's antics. Like someone surrendering because they're drained from the fight. The trip was Patty's first time meeting Mitch. They didn't hit it off well after Mitch said, "Do you need to have that annoying ringtone on?"

Mitch pouted over anything that didn't go his way. We ate where he wanted to eat and went where he wanted to go. I posted a sunset photo on Facebook and he sulked after he saw it. "You didn't say that you were here with me," he whined. He blindsided me with accusations of looking at other men. "You had to have seen that guy, he was looking right at you. I know you were looking at him." I blankly stared at him, not quite believing what I heard.

He demanded to know what I fantasized about. The question wasn't asked in a hey-what're-your-fantasies-let's-have-some-fun sort of way. He was demeaning and accusatory. "You slept with all those guys when you were young. I need to know that you're thinking about only me."

What in the holy fuck?

I had a promiscuous streak as a teen and had shared that with him a while back. I thought we were being transparent and sharing some of our less-than-stellar moments. Mitch apparently never had a less-than-stellar moment in his life. But he collected information on other people's life struggles and used it as an emotional weapon.

"My private thoughts are none of your business," I said. I wanted to go home. I'm done with this idiot, I thought. But home was thousands of miles over the ocean.

SQUATTER

    Mitch planned a hike for the four of us along the Kalalau Trail to Hanakapiai Beach, a secluded beach only accessible by foot. The Kalalau Trail was a treacherous trail along the sheer cliffs of the Nepali Coast, making it one of the most dangerous hikes in the world. The difficult hike to the beach and back would be a half-day adventure if we wanted to include time at the beach and be able to hike at a speed Martin's leg could handle.

    Anxious that Mitch didn't get us to the trail until one in the afternoon, I said, "Isn't it getting kinda late to start this?" Sunset in early March would be around 6:30.

    "There's plenty of time. I know what I'm doing." Mitch slammed the car door shut. He didn't like his decisions questioned.

    We were the only hikers heading out that late in the day. Returning hikers passed us saying things like, "You're all just gettin' started?" or "You'll never make it back by dark." Mitch was unconcerned. My irritation grew, and I found it difficult to enjoy the golden sand of Hanakapiai Beach. We weren't far into our return hike when the sun came to rest on the ocean horizon. We navigated the cliffs and slippery, mud-covered rocks with caution yet fully aware of the need to make good time. Martin began limping which slowed our progress.

    The sun disappeared below the horizon. Twilight didn't offer much light through the trees. I turned on my cell phone flashlight and shone it on the trail in front of Martin, who struggled to move along at a hobble. "Here–gimme your pack, Martin," Patty said, to make things easier for him. They were more than fifteen years my senior and the right thing to do was help them navigate.

Mitch disappeared down the trail. I'd made the mistake of trusting someone else with my safety. I knew nothing about that level of hiking preparedness. Now here I was, navigating cliffs overlooking a dark ocean with a limping man while my new boyfriend, who had multiple times poetically professed that he would risk his life to ensure my safety, was nowhere in sight.

If we didn't make it down by total darkness, we'd have to spend the night up there. Cell phone flashlights wouldn't offer enough light once twilight ended to safely illuminate the trail where one wrong step could be your last. Footsteps approached us from behind. A young couple with two powerful flashlights gained on us. "It'll be pitch black soon," one of them said with concern. "Here," the other one held out their flashlight. "Take one of ours and leave it at the trailhead when you're finished." We gratefully accepted and thanked them. They disappeared as quickly as they came upon us.

Out of the darkness, Mitch's voice boomed from down the trail, "LEAVE HIM AND COME DOWN HERE!"

"Martin needs help, we stay together," I yelled back. Anger boiled inside me. We were at a standstill. Mitch seethed at the fact that I helped his brother. Throughout the trip, I sensed a strange dynamic between them. To avoid more tantrums or delay, I caved in. Martin stood silent and unphased by Mitch's request. I handed Patty the powerful flashlight and headed down by Mitch. "Come on…go faster," he fumed when I refused to go at a pace where we would lose sight of Martin and Patty's light. We all made it down the trail and drove back to the timeshare in strained silence.

Mitch later insisted that my memory of what happened on the Kalalau Trail was faulty and that he bore no responsibility for us being out there after dark. In fact, he said his plan was to go on ahead and retrieve headlamps that were left in the car. Doesn't a good leader tell the rest of the group the plan? I thought. Doesn't an experienced outdoorsman already have headlamps with them? I barely spoke to him during the entire flight home.

After arriving home, I did what any sane person would do. I broke up with him. I wanted to break up in person after my work stretch at the hospital. He bombarded me with texts and emails. I woke up those work mornings to strings of emails sent throughout the night. I'd had enough. I sent what I thought was a well-crafted, mature email ending the relationship and why I felt forced into doing it via email.

I was stunned by his blunt response.

Slut, Whore, it's all the same. No man will ever be faithful to you because your breasts are so small.

His use of correct anatomical vocabulary coupled with vile name calling was perplexing. A stand-up guy one moment and a villain the next. A tantalizing jellyfish enticing you in, only to deliver a sting.

That's who Mitch was.

* * *

After Hawaii, Mitch sent a tidal wave of texts, emails and gifts. Apologies, stories of painful life events that he endured and reflections of his daily life like an interesting tree he saw on a walk or a yard project he was working on. He even left a goofy voicemail pretending to order a pizza. "Yes, I'd like a large, thin crust with Italian sausage, black olives and mushrooms with green pepper on half…" his voice trailed off, and the call ended with his soft, endearing laughter. He lived fifteen minutes away and showed up at my door begging me to talk to him.

"Just one more hug?" His tender voice lured me in. Pushing for physical contact during a breakup was a tactic he would use in our on-again, off-again relationship cycle. He did that because it worked.

That was not the same Mitch from Hawaii. His gentle, loving nature returned, making me question my version of the trip. Maybe I missed some family dynamic between Mitch and his brother that triggered him. Maybe that was it. Because the man begging for a hug, looking vulnerable and lonely, was not the same man from Hawaii. People deserve second chances. Don't they?

I had been handling a snake and gotten bit. When my kids were little we watched the Crocodile Hunter handle all kinds of dangerous creatures. But even with the caution, love, and respect in which he handled those animals, in the end, one took his life. Mitch wouldn't take my life, but he would break my spirit.

2

There is something very wrong.
This relationship is intoxicating.
I feel bound to Mitch and can't let go.

My late husband had earned a living for us as a long-haul truck driver. His absence allowed me to build my own life. I loved the creativity of homeschooling our five children. I pursued hobbies such as photography with my kids as my subjects. I played piano at our nearby Methodist church and practiced at home while the kids played outside. We agreed on some parenting ideas. He was raised in Texas during the 1960s with a lot of freedom. I liked the idea of free-range kids. When our sons were sixteen and twelve, they went on a weeklong camping trip to South Dakota by themselves. We had carefully prepared everything they'd need: a notarized letter stating they had permission to be traveling in our van, a binder with state patrol phone numbers and maps, a credit card hidden in the van and confidence in their abilities. While some might not have agreed with our style, it's what we did.

As I entered my forties, the Band-Aid of a busy family life could no longer conceal the unbearable pain of being with someone I didn't love. The trapped feeling became overwhelming. We were living apart during the last four years of his life. My husband moved out and rented a little house on our same block so the kids could come and go as they pleased. He got sick during that time and was unable to continue working. Those years were filled with nursing school, dealing with his cancer, and the stresses of an uprooted life. I got thrust into the role of provider after spending over two decades as a stay-at-home mom.

Ten months after my husband's death, I felt ready to move forward in choosing someone my forty-nine-year-old self wanted. I hoped for a new chance at love.

Since my marriage to my late husband had not been a close one, sex was to keep the peace and grow a family. I did it because that's what you do. Intimacy with Mitch, by contrast, intoxicated me. I gave my soul to him on those nights and at times we both shed tears at the intensity of it all. Those moments were what bonded me to him. It was the magnet that would keep me coming back again and again. For the first time in my life, I felt loved.

Mitch planned our trip to Isle Royale for early June 2018. He taught me about being in the backcountry: what to wear, what to eat, and how to use a compass. He taught me to read a topographic map. He showed me how to make GPS waypoints and use tracking tape while bushwhacking. "I'll take you to Sargent Lake for a day," he said.

I wanted to paddle the secret canoe on the wild lake that few humans had ever seen. And I did. We ducked off the Island's main trail and bushwhacked to Sargent Lake. Sure enough, concealed under a tarp in the thick forest, was the secret canoe. "Tada!" Mitch said, revealing the treasured canoe he worked so hard to hide. Within minutes we were on the water. I sat naked on its bow, soaking up the June sunshine as we drifted along in a wilderness paradise. "I'll bring you back here to camp someday. We'll have all of this to ourselves," he said as he gestured to the surrounding wilderness. The King of Isle Royale surveying his kingdom. I wanted that. And I needed Mitch in order to do it.

In addition to Sargent Lake's hidden canoe, Mitch had brought along a canoe on the ferry that would be our transportation around the island. Glorious island sunrises and sunsets lit up the sky. Moose swam across the water. Mitch had endless patience as he taught me to fish. My new-found love for the rugged island couldn't be dimmed even when Mitch threw a fit over a pair of underwear I hung out to dry. "A ranger could walk by and see that," he said. "You must want him to see it."

Mitch always presumed to know what I was thinking.

* * *

I took gradual, subtle steps in an unhealthy direction. In my desire to please Mitch, I accommodated his clothing demands. I guarded my speech, mannerisms and eye contact around other men, so as not to set him off. I was too smart for this. I was a nurse. I owned a home. I had taught my kids to read. I was aware it was happening, but yet I wasn't. The emotional whiplash of going from mountaintop highs to dark, spirit-crushing lows acted like a poisonous gas. The more I breathed in, the foggier things became. Like a carnival house of mirrors where you see your reflection. It's you, but yet it's not the real you. That's how life became with Mitch.

He always found reasons why I didn't live up to his standards as to how a woman in an "exclusive relationship" should behave. "You're not doing it intentionally. It's a subconscious thing," he said. "You just don't know how to love a man." That made it impossible to defend myself. He implied that my character was so flawed that I wasn't even aware of it. But, of course, he was.

He labeled me as having an attachment disorder after I shared with him that my mom had trouble caring for me as an infant. He could have been right. I definitely didn't have a track record of healthy relationships with men. "I'm willing to love you anyway," he said. "No one will ever love you like I do." He often let me know that he was "special" and not like other people. I should be glad he was with someone like me. "You only have a mediocre high school education and just a nursing degree beyond that," he sneered. He had gone to some fancy-pants high school. Shaming was his modus operandi.

Once, when I was at work, he sent me a photo of a tape measure stretched across my front yard, from my porch to the sidewalk. "This is how close you are to men walking down the sidewalk while you sit on your porch with no bra."

Underneath my work scrubs I wore long-sleeved shirts with a tiny, ribboned flower at the neck seam. Mitch cut off the flowers from the shirts, "Those flowers give the subtle message of intimacy to other men." He stole two of my t-shirts. "They were too fitted. I ripped them apart and used them to wipe up oil in my garage," he said.

Mitch became hyper-focused on my promiscuous teen streak and couldn't let it go. Did I still know them? Were they men he knew? We passed a construction worker on the side of the road. "You looked at him. He looks about your age. Is he one?" Mitch asked. Servers, co-workers, church members. Any male was suspect. He said I had been a whore, and he looked for any reason to prove it was still true.

Turmoil ensued over the most mundane of actions. I never knew when it was coming. He picked me up after work once. I got in the car and he said, "You flipped your hair while walking across the parking lot." He scrutinized every smile, glance, hair flip and tone of voice. What was right one day, was wrong the next. What confused me was that I thought abusers were monstrous, horrible people that could be easily picked out of a crowd. Like the playground bully. Everyone knows who it is. But Mitch's outer shell, most of the time, was a gentle demeanor.

Mitch helped me out with things a single woman often struggles to do on her own. He showed up to help me on one of our 'off' times when my car wouldn't start. He fixed things around my house. He sawed up fallen branches in my yard and neatly stacked them. He took me on my first backpacking trip to Pictured Rocks National Lakeshore and carried more than his share to ensure my pack wasn't too heavy for my body size.

That was the person I loved.

But that side of him didn't last. My spirit was breaking. But I couldn't let go. Living in a constant state of emotional chaos destabilized me and impeded my ability to think rationally. Marriage was a subject we talked about since the early months of our relationship. He often blamed his erratic behavior on his feelings of uncertainty about our future. "Once we're married I'll feel better," he said.

I fell into the raging river of our life together and was swept along, unable to pull myself out of its powerful current. We planned to be married on Groundhog Day, February 2, 2019. We never had an actual engagement moment or a ring. The river's current hurtled us in that direction. As we made plans for the small ceremony, conflict tore through my gut. I couldn't leave him, but I also couldn't cross the line into marriage. Mitch wore his I'm-a-great-guy facade with my kids, but they kept an emotional distance. I had received the nasty email he sent after Hawaii while I was with my daughter-in-law and had shown it to her. The other kids eventually learned about it. They weren't so keen on the second chances idea. Everything else that transpired between Mitch and I was private. The thought of others knowing was too embarrassing. How could another relationship fail again? The humorous and light face that he presented to others made the situation easy to hide.

I spent time with Mitch separately from my kids. Liz and Grace were polite when he was around the house, but distant with him. I spent special time with them going to dinner theater shows or getting coffee. The times I spent adventuring with Mitch, they had their grandparents and our next-door neighbor of twenty-five years to look in on them. Often, they'd visit their brother's family in Minnesota. I regularly spent a few days each month in the Twin Cities visiting two of my adult kids: my oldest, Jory, his wife and their two kids, and my daughter, Anna. They, understandably, weren't interested in connecting with Mitch, and I also didn't want him along. I made several trips to California to visit my second son, John, who was in the Marine Corps. Some of the best moments of my life were spent hiking in the desert with him. Deep down, I knew Mitch wasn't right for me. I wanted to enjoy my kids without him. Marrying him would be disastrous.

Two months before the wedding, Mitch and I flew to Arizona so I could meet his son who would not be attending our wedding. A tense energy divided them. Mitch's son spoke in flat, uninterested tones. Mitch acted like it wasn't happening and kept on with his cheery, lighthearted way. His son had cats, which triggered asthma for me, so Mitch, and I stayed at an Airbnb condo. We would share one night of our stay with another person. Unfortunately, that person was male. "You put that tinted Chapstick on to impress him, didn't you?" Mitch said. He wouldn't let me use the shared kitchen alone while the man was there. Thankfully, the guy left for the day.

Our Airbnb host left a welcome gift of wine on the counter. And again, unfortunately, the wine's name was Ménage à Trois. Mitch furiously claimed that our host hinted at a threesome between her guests. "This is disgusting!" he said. He picked up the bottle and stared at it. I knew what he was going to do. I wanted to disappear into the floor.

Time halted. The seconds ticked by in slow motion, like a frame-by-frame movie clip. I read somewhere that we often remember traumatic incidents in slow motion because it's a neurological coping mechanism. Our fight-or-flight response gears up. Nausea seized my stomach as I anticipated the damage that was coming.

Mitch raised the bottle over his head and threw it like a football across the kitchen. I stood frozen while the bottle flew through the air. By the grace of God, it ricocheted off of the counter's rounded edge and wildly spun across the countertop. I threw myself over the spinning bottle to stop its momentum.

The wedding was off.

* * *

But we weren't off. Oh, we were off for a while after Arizona. We backed out of the house we were going to buy and lost our earnest money. I made multiple break-up attempts, but always got sucked back in. So the cycle continued. Sometimes we went through the cycle in the course of a day. I was a kid screaming to get off the merry-go-round only to turn back and yell, "Again!" Like the saying goes, you play stupid games, you win stupid prizes. I found it impossible to remove Mitch from my life.

In June of 2019, we took our second trip to Isle Royale. Mitch hoped we would still get married someday. "We just had some rough patches," he said while starting up the camp stove for breakfast at Isle Royale's Duncan Bay. "Things would be different if we were married." Later that afternoon while on a hike, Mitch brought up the subject of photos he didn't like that I posted on Facebook. "Sooooo…you think posting that jumping photo of you is appropriate?" he asked, as if he plucked the subject off of a tree as we walked by.

I stopped on the trail and faced him. "I will never marry you." He turned around and headed down the trail acting like he never heard me.

* * *

After we returned from Isle Royale, I wanted to end the relationship for good. No more merry-go-round. No more on-again, off-again. An online friend wrote, *These kinds of relationships are hard to leave and are as addictive as any drug.*

What kind of relationships? Addictive? How can someone be addicted to a person? I thought. She went on to explain that in order to successfully end relationships with people like Mitch, you have to sever contact with them. All contact. *The dynamics of the relationship make it easy for them to suck you back in. Even negative contact, such as arguing with them, is contact, and they thrive on it*, she wrote. Sounds kind of drastic, I thought. I wish he'd just accept breaking up like a normal person. But I wasn't dealing with normal.

I texted Mitch that we were done. In-person breakups never worked as he often refused to leave my house. I blocked him from texting, calling, and Facebook. But email couldn't truly be blocked. A sender could be blocked from coming to an inbox, but it's diverted to the spam folder. Mitch's emails poured into my spam folder. I couldn't help but look. And respond. Ignoring someone seemed unnatural and rude.

I'm sick to my stomach over the way you speak to me, I need you to stop contacting me, I emailed. *I'm getting to the point that I'm going to consider a restraining order for this to be done.*

He continued to send gifts and cards along with endless emails. He knew I wouldn't go through with a restraining order. You see, Mitch was an attorney. I wouldn't want to face him in court. His comfort zone. And he knew it.

In mid-September 2019, after he left another gift at my door, I went to the police department and talked with a female officer. "Mitch has a strong personality, and I can't get him to stop contacting me." She called Mitch as I sat at the table across from her. She told him to end contact. Then she turned to me and said, "Don't you contact him either." Relieved, I left the police department, ready to take on my new-found freedom.

I was determined not to contact him again.

3

How do we get into such complicated situations?
I have no excuse.
I got here by my own choice.

I planned my first solo camping trip days after leaving the police station. I didn't want the outdoor adventures to end. Joining hiking and camping groups were an option, but being a nurse, I didn't have a Monday through Friday work life with weekends off. And most of the organized outdoor groups were in southeastern Wisconsin. That was okay, I wasn't a group person anyway. If I was going to continue to experience the outdoors, I needed to learn to do it myself. My new gear from a cool outdoorsy store arrived on my doorstep, and I was ready to go.

But where?

I chose Rock Island State Park, a tiny Lake Michigan island off the tip of Door County–Wisconsin's "thumb". Two ferry rides were needed to reach the island: a car ferry to the larger Washington Island, followed by a passenger-only ferry to Rock Island. Not having my car ensured that I couldn't bail. I'd have to see it through.

After a rainy, four-hour drive, I arrived at the tip of Door County and pulled in line behind the other vehicles. The ferry to Washington Island ran hourly, on a first come first serve basis. The Rock Island ferry didn't run as often. I hoped to make the midday passage to Rock Island in order to have the afternoon to set up camp and explore.

Heavy clouds hung low after the morning's rain. A box truck rolled onto the ferry without room behind it for me. I sighed and prepared to wait for the next ferry. The truck inched forward with guidance from a dock worker. After inspecting the space behind it, the worker waved me on and I squeezed in. Made it.

I drove across Washington Island and arrived at the Rock Island Ferry parking with forty-five minutes to spare. Adjacent to the parking lot, a sign reading Jackson Harbor Soup caught my attention. I could use lunch, I thought. I entered the barn-shaped building, choosing a table with a view of Lake Michigan. Rock Island sat on the water's horizon a mile away. The tables quickly filled. The casual greetings between patrons hinted that the harbor eatery was a popular, local lunch stop. I swallowed my first bite of chili when a gray-haired lady ambled up to my table. "May I join you?" she asked with a warm smile. I welcomed her to sit down.

"I'm Blueberry, The Butterfly Lady, but you can call me Blueberry," she said while pulling out the chair across from me. "I hatch butterflies here on the Island and voila…" she paused with dramatic flair, "before I knew it, I became the Butterfly Lady."

"I'm waiting for the next passenger ferry," I said, tapping my phone to check the time.

"So what brings you to Rock Island?" she asked, diving into her lunch.

"I'm going on my first solo camping trip."

"Oh my goodness! How exciting!" she said in between bites. "You'll be fine, but I insist that you add my name to your phone contacts. There should be cell service at the dock. If you have any trouble, I'll come for you in my boat."

I thanked her, said goodbye and headed to the ferry dock at the other end of the parking lot.

I sat on a bench in the small boat as it rose and fell with the waves, my body yielding to the motion. The nippy September wind forced wisps of hair loose from under my baseball cap. I pushed back the strands and watched the island's massive stone boathouse come into view. Lake Michigan's choppy waves swept over the Rock Island dock as the boat eased its way alongside it. I stepped off the ferry in between crashing waves, attempting to make it to shore with dry legs and feet. Being stuck wearing damp hiking boots for a few days wasn't appealing.

With a dramatic flair, I exhaled and said, "Alright, let's do this." But there was no us.

I was alone.

I picked up my pack and followed the trail into the woods. The island sat quiet in late September's off-season. Day trippers and weekend campers would still come to hike and tour the island's lighthouse, but even they would be few in numbers. I lugged my pack the half-mile to the campground, picked a site and set up my tent. A sandy beach spanned the shoreline, steps away from my site. This is all mine, I thought, running down to the sand. I spent the rest of the day exploring the beach. The afternoon shadows lengthened.

I grabbed my water bag and walked back across the island to the spigot near the dock. A young couple from the ferry stood by the spigot, waiting for their bottles to fill. They were a comforting sight as I hadn't seen anyone all afternoon. I really wanted to say, "Oh boy, am I glad to see you guys… it's gonna get lonely out here in the dark…so could we hang out a bit? Maybe a cozy campfire and s'mores?" But I returned their polite hello before they walked away and were swallowed up by the wooded island. The last ferry of the day pulled away from the dock. I stood alone as the sun shone low in the sky.

Nearby, the stone boathouse stood like an abandoned, ancient ruin. A testimony to a time when quality craftsmanship and grandeur were seen even in remote settings. I walked up its steps and found the door unlocked, welcoming visitors at any hour. I explored its museum to occupy my mind.

After the sun dipped behind the distant Washington Island, I carried my water back into the woods. The wind and waves roared beyond the trees. Even on a Great Lakes island this small, the weather could drastically vary. Calm on one side. Fierce on the other.

Loneliness percolated in my chest as daylight faded. I missed being with someone in charge. During our adventures, Mitch had been the leader and I was the follower. I was okay with that. Now he was gone and I was on my own.

"Why did you have to be such an ass?!" I vented to an audience of trees as twilight faded. "Now I'm stuck out here doing this myself!" Tears fell and I blinked hard.

Back at my site, wet wood from the morning's rain kept my fire from being a success. I put on my headlamp and turned my attention to my camp stove. I poured boiling water into my dried dinner and stepped down to the beach. I ate while watching the stars take their place for the night.

The trip wasn't only about learning to do things myself. I needed to overcome my fear of the dark woods. Whenever I had to get up in the night to pee, Mitch had been there. A protector in the darkness. Kids believed monsters lived under their beds. As adults, we know better.

But do we?

Or do we transfer those under-the-bed-monster fears to other places like the woods at night? The best way to handle my fear of the dark woods was to not look out into it. Stay focused on the task at hand. When nature called, I kept my eyes on where the headlamp illuminated. I slept well my first night camping alone. The wind and waves were my constant companions until sunrise.

Pride burst from every pore in my body the next day. I had done it. My first night camping alone. I hiked with joyous energy around the island and toured the lighthouse. But as the day's light faded, the uneasiness returned. Fears aren't eliminated overnight. It would be a work in progress. I savored the warmth of the fire built by my hands and then prepared for bed. "Focus on what's in front of me," I said to myself.

Late the following morning, I made the return trip on the passenger ferry, feeling triumphant as it glided through the calm Lake Michigan waters. On the drive home, I chose the song, "I Will Survive," to blare on repeat.

* * *

After returning from Rock Island, I checked my spam email every day during that first no-contact attempt. I don't know why. Habit maybe. I knew Mitch wouldn't heed the officer's warning. Two weeks later, he sent me a long email detailing the woes of his childhood and why he was the way he was. I didn't respond, but I lit up at the sight of his name. Like lightning flashed through my brain.

Determined to stick with no-contact, I delved into podcasts and books about psychology and relationships. I wanted to understand our situation. I saw us in the descriptions as I read and listened. But it was difficult for me to accept that Mitch's behavior was abusive. Maybe because his gentle side stood in such stark contrast. Maybe it wasn't exactly us in the descriptions. Kinda sort of, but not really. I couldn't see the obvious. I naively thought he needed this information. Maybe if he learned about it, he would get help. If he read it, he would want therapy.

Like a fool, I sent him a link ten days after he emailed me, no message attached. That's all it took to reopen communication between us. I'd blown it. I'd done the exact opposite of what the officer had told me to do. How could I have been so stupid? The mess to come would be my fault. And I would have to handle it on my own.

* * *

I refused to see Mitch regularly. No traveling together. No coming to my house. But I longed for the physical intimacy we had shared. That's when he was the person I loved. The vile words and demeaning accusations fell away in those hours. I agreed to see him once in a while. But I insisted it be at his house because I didn't want anyone to know. I didn't know how I'd explain to my kids why I would continue seeing someone who had treated me badly.

In the two years I had known him, I had never spent time inside his home, mere minutes from me. "Since the divorce, I had been so focused on other things that housekeeping got away from me. It's just really messy," he said early in our relationship to explain why I couldn't come over. I found that believable and didn't want to embarrass him. It's hard for me to admit that I planned to marry someone whose home I hadn't seen.

We met six weeks after that first no-contact attempt. With the promise of sex, he'd spent days cleaning up his bedroom and bathroom. I walked through the dimly lit living room and kitchen. The items in his house looked as if a moving truck had backed up to the door and tossed everything inside. A dilapidated back deck stood unused for possibly years. The living room flooring had been removed exposing the plywood. Stacks of items lay helter-skelter in the living room, indicating the floor wasn't a recent work in progress. The house's condition was far from a divorcé letting housekeeping get away from him. The chaos that he created in our relationship was reflected in his surroundings. Something deeper haunted Mitch. Yet, I didn't want to acknowledge what was right in front of me.

Once a month, we repeated a round and round cycle. We'd meet for sex. Afterwards, I'd say this wasn't a good idea. He'd convinced me otherwise. In between our meetups, I worked to build my confidence by creating experiences without Mitch. In January 2020, I left Grace to visit her oldest brother in the Twin Cities and hopped on a plane for a solo trip to Death Valley National Park. After landing in Las Vegas, I waited in line for my rental car. Posters of pickup trucks hung on the wall behind the counter. The stereotypical advertisements of tough trucks bounding through the wilderness. They emitted a powerful vibe that I couldn't resist.

"Can I upgrade to a truck?" I asked the clerk.

I headed west out of Las Vegas in a blue Nissan Frontier feeling like I could take on the world. No one messes with a badass behind the wheel of a pickup truck. Even a small one, right? Pahrump, Nevada was home base as I spent the days hiking in Death Valley, one of the harshest environments on Earth. Someplace easy wouldn't cut it for that solo trip. I needed to do hard things in tough places on my own. On the drive back to the airport, the emotional high from the thrill of having done that adventure alone brought me to tears. After arriving home, I hightailed it to my local Nissan dealer and drove away with my very own blue Frontier named Fiona–the first female 'F' name that came to mind to go with Frontier.

* * *

In February, I headed to the Porcupine Mountains of Michigan's Upper Peninsula for a two-night yurt stay. Another self-confidence building, solo adventure on the winter shore of Lake Superior. A few weeks later, in early March 2020, I took Fiona on a six-day road trip and ended up in the Nebraska Sandhills. The exhilaration of being free on the road with no real destination boosted my desire to let go of Mitch. I returned feeling certain I wouldn't see him again.

Immediately after returning from Nebraska, Covid changed our world. "What states did you drive through?" my nurse manager messaged. "Certain ones are on a quarantine list–we've got travel nurses who drove through Illinois to get here and now can't come to work." Fortunately, I had not driven through one of the listed states. Areas of the hospital transformed into Covid units. Liz continued to work at a nearby grocery store where lines grew long and people bought excess toilet paper. Grace was already homeschooled and had many online friends from around the country, so her world didn't change much. My older daughter, Anna, returned home from college in Minneapolis and got hired on the spot at Aldi. Regular visits to my son's family in Minnesota ceased. We masked up and faced an uncertain future.

In April, we were asked to stay close to home. I combed my county looking for places to hike on public land and county forests. Then I remembered the Ice Age Trail. It's gotta be nearby, I thought. I searched for an online trail map and sure enough, it went through my county.

 I had heard about the trail during my high school years, when we lived along the Wisconsin River in northern Wisconsin. After school, I would ride my bike to the nearby Grandfather Falls Dam. The dam, with its seven floodgates, spanned the river. Each gate created an eighty-nine-foot waterfall. When fully opened, the dam released a dramatic amount of water that roared over boulders pitting the riverbed below. I often explored a trail that followed along the river's edge. My mom told me it was the Ice Age Trail and that it wound through the state, highlighting geological features created by a long-ago ice age. I found it intriguing.

 At the age of twelve, I checked out the books, *A Walk Across America* and *The Walk West* by Peter Jenkins, from our library and devoured his stories. Those books enthralled me. My heart broke when Peter's dog, Cooper, died on the journey. When he met his wife, Barbara, I didn't like her butting into the story. But I laughed during the chapters in the second book where she recalled her version of the journey. Her female perspective gave a new side to the tale. A woman could do it, too. After those books ended, I flipped through picture books about the Appalachian Trail while the vinyl crackling melody of Aaron Copland's "Appalachian Spring" spun on a turntable. A walking adventure sounded wonderful.

* * *

I hadn't seen Mitch since February. The shelter in place request of those weeks made it easy to say no when he pressed to see me. I spent my free days in April of 2020 exploring the trail in my county. Early spring was Wisconsin's mud season. Endless mud and standing water defined the trail, which often ran through flooded lowland areas. After maneuvering through soggy woods, I gave up my boots and socks while the trail followed a flooded, grassy powerline right-of-way. After the initial sting of icy water on my skin, I gingerly moved through the standing water.

I turned fifty-two in mid-April, spending the afternoon exploring another trail segment. I passed some of the geological features that define the Ice Age Trail. The trail led up hills called kames created by mounds of sediment deposited by glacial ice. Little ponds known as kettles dotted the woods. Random giant boulders, called erratics, deposited by traveling ancient glacial ice appeared to grow out of the forest floor. As the sun set at the end of my birthday, Mitch had sent the ninth email of the day. During the night, he left gifts at my door, an assortment of items that escape my memory. Most likely teas, chocolates, food items and a card. His typical gift style.

By the end of April, I had explored over twenty miles of trail in my county. That didn't include the miles spent walking back to Fiona. I thought about how much of the trail I'd like to complete. Maybe I'd do the four hundred miles from my home county in north central Wisconsin to the Western Terminus in St. Croix at the state's border. The northern stretch. I wasn't sure about the logistics. Out-and-back hiking wasn't practical. I'd figure out something.

I had the brilliant idea to kick off my new goal of hiking to the Western Terminus with a bang. Rehike everything I had already done. Twenty-three-and-a-half miles in one day. I'd never hiked more than nine miles at one time before. How bad could it be? I thought. It's just walking. April 30, 2020, would mark the official start of my goal. I packed snacks, water, my Jetboil for morning coffee and extra socks.

Anna dropped me off at the Plover River segment at the county line minutes before sunrise. "Good luck, text me when you get close to Poplar Lane!" She waved and her car disappeared around the bend.

The morning sunbeams filtered through the trees, illuminating the carpet of ramps spread across the forest floor. The cliche that spring offers the hope of new beginnings felt true as I hoped for a life without Mitch. I made mid-morning coffee and ate a snack along the swollen Eau Claire River, still feeling pumped about the day. I ended up barefoot again, sloshing through the muddy mess. I hit the eight-mile mark and my bones ached. At twelve miles, my pace slowed.

At twenty miles, I was over it. The bones in my legs went from aching to downright painful. My backpack's waist strap rubbed against my hips. Lifting my shirt revealed flaming red skin. The tenderness grew worse with each step. My pack made a weird squeaking noise over my right shoulder. I couldn't tune it out. Mitch had stolen that Osprey backpack from me to "teach me a lesson" about some shortcoming he saw in me. He returned it after he found my late husband's military compass from Vietnam tucked in a pouch.

My second son, John, and I used the backpack on a Mojave Desert hike when I visited him at Twentynine Palms Marine Corps Base. He tucked his dad's compass in the pouch, and we forgot about it. Mitch claimed he didn't technically steal the pack since he was planning to return it. Supposedly, after I learned my lesson and he had made his self-righteous point. He said the word steal indicated permanence of possession on the part of the thief and that was not his intention. While that definition may be true, he said things like that to steer away from the core truth of a conversation. I attempted to tell him that he had no right to take my things. Instead of addressing my feelings about an issue, he'd rant about something else, like the technical definition of the word steal. And before I knew it, he'd be a mile away from the initial point of the attempted conversation. Mitch twisted things, which made it difficult to have a real conversation with him. I could go round and round with him all day and never get anywhere but exhausted. I assumed that he returned the pack after finding the compass because it wasn't good karma to steal from a deceased Vietnam veteran.

The pack's squeaking taunted me, and I couldn't stop hearing it. My legs throbbed deep in the bones. I groaned out loud. How much farther? Anna texted that she was at the Poplar Lane trailhead. It's gotta be close.

"SISSY!! ARE YOU OUT THERE?!" I hollered for her through the trees. I couldn't believe the intensity of my agony. "Oh, my gosh, where the freak is she?" I groaned and cursed through those last steps. Finally, I stumbled out of the woods onto Poplar Lane. Anna and her car were a beautiful sight. I collapsed in the front seat and muttered, "Oh my gosh, Sissy, take me home." I closed my eyes and dreamed of ordering a pizza.

4

*I am in love with who I WISH Mitch would be
and not who he really is.
I love a version of him that doesn't exist.*

Mitch emailed multiple times during that long day hike. Later that night, I wrote to him about my big hike, longing for his love and approval. I wanted to be heard by him. His response was, *Gosh, what an accomplishment, it was a beautiful day for it.* The normalness of that response fed my soul. That's how normal, happy couples interact. The couple in the grocery store. The couple on the plane. The couple doing yard work on Saturday morning. One says something about their day and the other shows interest. A partner gives praise and celebrates you. We hadn't seen each other in over two months. Even though deep down I knew his loving, kind emails were part of the game, they still impacted me. I longed for him to be something that he wasn't.

Two days after the big hike, I drove one county north to start a portion of the trail named the Underdown Segment after a local homesteader. I followed the trail to a lake surrounded by pine trees. The scene resembled Isle Royale with its peaked pines overlooking the water. I teared up at the thought of never being able to return. Attempting Isle Royale alone was beyond my skill level. I had to let it go.

SQUATTER

At the end of the day, I had hiked eight miles, but only covered four miles of the trail. Continuing to hike out and back wasn't practical. I did twice the work to gain half the accomplishment. I had another idea. A few days later, I convinced Liz to return with me. We left her vehicle at one trailhead and then drove to the other to start the hike. We covered hilly trail miles and a connecting road route for an eight-mile day. Liz was a good sport that day but she wasn't interested in doing the trail. She slipped in her Airpods and moved along. The two-car idea wouldn't carry me through to the Western Terminus.

I spent the next day, May 7, with Mitch at his home. Since last fall, I worked hard on letting go and yet, here I was. Again. The day's intimacy worked its magic and flooded me with emotion. After two-and-a-half years with Mitch, I intellectually knew nothing would change. I could voice the words, "Nothing will change," but my emotional mind couldn't rationally think through the mental fog and confusion those years created. Like an alcoholic who can't resist the next drink, I couldn't stop seeing Mitch.

* * *

I had an old, heavy Schwinn bike that was a hand-me-down from my dad. Bike shuttling was the answer. I could park Fiona, pedal to the other trailhead via a road route, lock up the bike, hike the trail, then drive back for it. But first, I had to get it into Fiona's five-foot bed. The bike wouldn't fit right and allow the tailgate to close. I unloaded and tried again. And again. I turned the handlebars one way, then the other. I kept trying. Finally, with the bike's front wheel turned just right, the tailgate closed.

I had paper maps and screenshots of the trail segments since cell service in northern Wisconsin could be sketchy.

I pedaled my first bike shuttle and was pretty pleased with myself. It was a bit hilly. But my new shuttling idea energized me. Within a few days, I burned through lots of miles.

The northern forest west of the Wisconsin River was a mysterious place to me during my high school years. In the 1980s, we lived on the river's east side along scenic Highway 107. I'd gaze at the dense forest across the river, believing it to be no-man's land. The Great Unknown. Heck, it could have been the tip of the Yukon for all my young self knew.

I savored the cool, early spring air while navigating the dense woods. Stepping on rocks jutting out of soggy ground kept my feet fairly dry. The trail led to the west bank of the Wisconsin River. For the first time, I viewed Grandfather Falls Dam from the opposite side of the river. The same impressive dam I explored as a kid, but from a different perspective. The dam hadn't changed. It couldn't change. My perspective had. Sort of like roaming through the grocery store, following the same route, week after week. If you change it up, you might see new items that you never noticed before. Our limited perspective is often not the whole picture. Could the trail change my perspective on other things as well?

* * *

Up before the sun, I loaded up my bike and headed back north. The Averill-Kelly Creek Wilderness segment and a portion of Newwood would make for an over ten-mile hiking day plus seven miles of biking. The county highway led to a dirt road as farm fields yielded to woods. The bars on my phone disappeared. Old camping trailers nestled amongst the trees were the only signs that people came to those woods.

SQUATTER

I pulled Fiona into the grassy trailhead parking lot as the early morning sun beamed through the bare trees. Before leaving home, I'd tossed an extra pair of boots into the backseat, preparing for a soggy trail from the recent snow melt and heavy rain. The woods gave off a crisp, fresh energy from the passing of another winter. The day's temperature would reach the forties. I put on my puffy jacket and daypack. The lack of cell service freed me from Mitch's emails for the day. Being cut off felt good.

My style was to bike first, then hike. That way, after hiking, when my bones ached, I'd be done. Or if my bike got stolen or a tire went flat, I wouldn't be stuck. I hopped on my bike and pedaled down a dirt road that was soft from spring thaw. My bike was not a fancy, lightweight deal. I pushed the rusty pedals through the soft dirt as my backpack shifted side to side with each exertion. Forty-five minutes and five miles later I let out a heavy sigh as I coasted into the opposite trailhead on Burma Road. Five miles in forty-five minutes? How embarrassing, I thought as I locked my bike to a tree. I breathed in the rich aroma of last autumn's wet leaves thawing after a winter submerged in snow and followed the yellow blazes marking the trail into the woods.

An endless swamp stretched across the forest floor. Few hikers came to the area to wear down a path. The mucky water hid the slightest evidence that anyone had come before me. The yellow blazes became navigation beacons on the submerged trail. I hopped onto tufts of grass and fallen branches, attempting to stay dry as I traveled from blaze to blaze. Keeping sight of the yellow markings was the only way out of the woods.

Up ahead, the trail disappeared into a shallow stream. Ooooo, a stream crossing for an added touch of adventure.

How quaint. Although the stream only needed a few steps to cross, it was deep enough to submerge my feet. I didn't know other hikers left their boots on to plow through water. It made sense to me to go barefoot if I could see the creek bottom. Leaning up against a tree, I peeled off my boots and socks. I grimaced as the icy water stung my toes. The initial sting turned to invigoration after arriving on the other side.

The swollen forest floor eventually gave way to drier ground with spotty mucky areas. I picked up my pace. Up ahead, the trail disappeared into another creek, a little deeper than the last one, but the bottom was still visible. I walked along the creek, pushing through thick brush that snagged my hair, seeking a shallower crossing. No luck.

Once again I took off my boots and winced as the water swirled upwards past my ankles. On the creek bank, I dried my feet and brushed off dirt before shoving them back in my boots. So much fuss to only gain a few yards. Back on the trail for mere steps, I rounded a corner and came to another dead end of water. "What the heck kinda trail is this?" I fumed. Who makes a trail through all this water? I literally put on my boots two minutes ago. I rolled my eyes and huffed a sigh of indignation.

A narrow but swiftly moving river blocked my path. *Maybe the trail stays on this side of the river?* I thought, searching the riverbank for evidence of the trail. The yellow blaze on the other side let me know that crossing the river was the way. I weighed my options. I had been on the trail for two hours and wasn't turning back. The end must be near. I studied the river and couldn't see the bottom. Jagged rocks could be hiding under that rushing water. I could be knocked off balance and get my foot stuck. Or broken. The best option was to cross in my boots and deal with soaked feet until I reached Fiona.

I rolled up my pant legs and stepped into the frigid river. "Ahhh!!" I yelled as the river rose to my bare thighs. The water stung like tiny needles scraping past my skin. I took deep, controlled breaths to stay focused. Holding my arms out for balance, I blindly placed each foot firmly on the river's bottom to resist being knocked over by the current. My heavy feet slogged onto the muddy bank. "Oh my gosh! That was painfully cold!" I rolled down my wet pants over my numb legs and hit the trail at a fast pace to generate heat. Water oozed from my boots with each step, creating a rhythmic squishing sound that accompanied me the rest of the way.

I exited the Averill-Kelly Creek segment feeling as radiant as the blue sky above me. I had done another hard thing on my own. I didn't need someone to save the day or make the decisions. After a short road walk back to Fiona, I exchanged my wet boots for dry ones, boiled water in my Jetboil for coffee and sat on the tailgate to eat a sandwich.

Maybe it would be a good idea to buy that guidebook I saw on the trail's website. I would later read in the Ice Age Trail Guidebook that the three crossings were Kelly Creek–the cute little trout stream, Averill Creek and the New Wood River. The book warned that the river could be treacherous during excessively wet periods.

After lunch, I drove down the dirt road to fetch my bike for part two of the day. A porcupine emerged from the tall, roadside grass. I stopped and took his photo as he passed in front of Fiona, switching my phone to video, as he waddled into the woods.

I returned to the same trailhead and hopped onto my bike, pedaling in the opposite direction. A rutted and mucky road made for an even more difficult ride than the morning's. My tires sank into a mud pit that spanned the road and stretched into the woods. I slipped off the bike seat and my boots sloshed into the mud. I pushed the old Schwinn through the muck and up a hill.

After locking my bike to the trailhead sign, I entered the Newwood segment that traversed through the New Wood State Wildlife Area. The different spellings didn't escape me. I later learned that both spellings were part of the area's history. The one-word spelling, according to locals, was the historical spelling referring back to when the area was a source of new wood for logging during the late 1800s. The two-word spelling became the official name after fires in the 1930s burned much of the area and new wood growth emerged. Numerous pines towered over the trail. They had escaped the logging era due to their small size at the time. I passed under their canopy and walked along a ridge, overlooking a river. I bet that's the river I crossed, I thought.

That evening, while soaking in my tub, I swiped through the day's photos, stopping at the porcupine. The cute, little guy who crossed the road. But something odd was in the photo. A black blob. I zoomed in on the photo. I squinted. The blob was farther down the road from the porcupine.

What the heck? No way. A black bear! Right in front of me. And I never saw him. I laughed in amazement at the sheer coincidence of capturing both creatures in one photo. My first bear encounter while doing the trail…and I missed it.

I think there's a life lesson in there somewhere.

5

*My first camping adventure on the trail
kept my mind off Mitch.
I think doing the whole trail
would be good for me.*

The spring days warmed, stirring an urge to camp. I checked out the trail map of the neighboring county to the west in my newly purchased Ice Age Trail Guidebook. The fourteen-and-a-half-mile Wood Lake segment, just over the county line, would be perfect for my first overnight on the trail. Completing the long, winding segment alone would require some piecing together. After the water crossings on the Averill-Kelly Creek segment, I bought Crocs at Fleet Farm. They weighed almost nothing and easily clipped to my backpack.

Taylor County campgrounds were some of the few that had reopened since April's lockdown. I rolled into Wood Lake County Park in the late afternoon. Kids climbed on the playground equipment and rode their bikes. Couples strolled alongside the road. Dads, wearing hoodies and holding beers, stoked fires for yummy dinners. With everything closed and not much to do, there was a rush on camping. A perfectly wonderful thing to do. But the busy campground wasn't the experience I longed for. I checked Google Maps and zoomed in on the area. The Taylor County Forest was a couple of miles away.

The dirt road into the forest led to a worn campground sign stating, "Free camping before Memorial Day." I couldn't believe my good fortune. I picked a site and set up my tent. My tent. My camping stuff. My adventure. No more being along for the ride on Mitch's adventures.

I combed the woods for fallen branches to saw up for a fire, determined not to focus on how much I'd appreciate a male partner at that moment. When I lugged the branches to my site and dropped them near the fire pit, something on the ground, tucked alongside the fire ring, caught my attention. An anxious robin chirped from a nearby tree. On the ground next to the metal, sat a nest containing two blue eggs. Are you kidding me? A robin's nest on the ground? There's no way these eggs will survive, I thought, and gawked at it while Mama Robin continued her scolding from above.

I thought of Martha Robin, who built a nest in the bend of my front porch's wreath every spring. That created tension between Martha and me. I wanted to sit on my porch, and she wanted to sit on my wreath. I kept my movements slow and gentle. No sudden moves. She eventually accepted my presence on the porch. I even took a selfie with Martha perched in her nest a few feet behind me as proof of our unusual friendship. All that changed one morning after her babies had hatched. While she was out looking for worms, I crept over to her nest to snap a picture. As I hovered over the nest with my phone, a nearby flutter made me look over my shoulder. Martha stood on the porch, glaring at me.

She caught me. I eased back to my rocking chair. She wasn't having it. She dive-bombed me, screeching and squawking. "Martha! It's me!" I exclaimed while covering my head with my hands. But the spell had been broken and she never accepted me on the front porch again.

Now, another mama robin was mad at me. I debated what to do. I just set up my tent. She's gonna lose these eggs anyway. This is a good site. I sighed, shook my head, and pulled up the tent stakes. Oh well. The new site was closer to the water pump anyway.

The night's forecast called for clear skies, enticing me to sleep without the tent's rainfly. I snuggled into my sleeping bag well before the stars made their appearance and relished the freedom from cell service. The forest's peepers serenaded me to sleep under a fading orange sky.

Hours later, I awoke to darkness. The forest stood mute and still. But there was something. The sky. The stars were calling. Stirring in my bag, I groped for my glasses and gazed upward. Shining beacons embedded in dark velvet pulsated above me. Alone in the Taylor County Forest, a mere speck in the universe, the company of stars comforted me. Star friends saying, "You got this."

At first light, mosquitoes swarmed the soggy forest floor surrounding my campsite. I packed up camp and drove back to Wood Lake for breakfast, hoping the open grassy area by the beach would be less buggy. I studied the trail map over oatmeal and coffee as the sun rose over Wood Lake. With my pant legs tucked into my socks to keep out ticks, I hit the trail.

Something rustled in the woods and I turned toward the noise. A porcupine scurried up a tree. He paused long enough to have his photo taken before disappearing to the other side of the trunk for his ascent. While on a logging road, two deer ambled my way. They didn't notice me in the shade as they strolled along. The larger one finally caught sight of me and stopped. She bobbed her head up and down while stomping her foot. She wanted me out of her way. I patiently waited until they retreated into the woods.

After lunch on Fiona's tailgate, I turned onto Bear Avenue to park for a shorter afternoon bike shuttle and hike. The word avenue suggested civilization: houses, people, shops along paved streets. But someone decided that a remote dirt road through a county forest–pretty much devoid of humans should be christened an avenue. Bear gave it a bit of a wild vibe, but Bear Road would be more straightforward, letting you know what to expect. A humongous pile of bear poop sat in the middle of the road. I bet they don't see that on New York's Fifth Avenue.

The county forest would be my home for another night. After setting up camp at the same site, I went in search of firewood and to check on the mama robin. The fire ring nest was destroyed. Broken, blue, egg shells lay scattered on the ground. Awww…poor mama. Did birds feel loss in the same way we did? Did she robotically set about creating a new nest? Or did her heart feel heavy? At least I hadn't been the cause of her stress. I hauled back my load and started a good fire. The smoke kept away the mosquitoes enough for me to enjoy a dehydrated beef stroganoff dinner. It would be another night without the rainfly, under the stars.

My morning bike shuttle took me back down Bear Avenue. A woman, tending a farmyard garden, stood and waved as I passed fields and entered the woods. After forty minutes of heavy pedaling on loose gravel and walking my bike up a long hill, I made it and locked my bike to a logging road gate. The morning sun illuminated the iridescent, spring green of budding trees. In between patches of the

SQUATTER

greening forest floor stood mud and water. Muck was the theme of the morning. I was thankful for my new Crocs.

The battle of the bugs and water was worth it after seeing three impressive beaver dams, one spanning over a hundred feet creating the boundary of a pond. I stopped at a worn, informational sign erected in the middle of the woods marking the site of Camp #7, one of twenty-eight such logging camps owned by the Rib Lake Lumber Company. Between 1910 and 1914, sixty men lived and worked at that spot. A railroad line even accessed the camp. But all that bustle and logging life had disappeared. Nothing remained but odd mounds on the forest floor as nature reclaimed the site.

I finished the Wood Lake segment and picked up the old Schwinn on Bear Avenue and parked for lunch. Thinking a quick tick check would be a good idea, I bent over to check underneath the flap of my zip-off-at-the-knee pants. I lifted the flap and flinched. "Ick!!" Dozens and dozens of ticks, packed on top of each other, squiggled along the zippers of both legs.

I jumped out of my pants right there on Bear Avenue and stood in my underwear alongside Fiona. With my face scrunched in disgust, I brushed off the nasty things, gave my pants a shake and tossed them into Fiona's bed before digging out my other pair. Lesson learned. I never wore zip-off pants on the trail again.

Enough time remained in the day to squeeze in the nearly four-mile Timberland Wilderness segment. But reaching it posed a bit of a problem. Both of the Timberland Wilderness's trailheads were on Tower Road as the segment basically paralleled the road. And Tower Road was on the other side of the county forest. Accessing it would mean a long drive around the forest's borders on county roads–roads with official sounding names like Highway M. There had to be another way.

I studied the map in the guidebook. Wilderness Avenue cut through the county forest. In parentheses, were the words, primitive road. Wilderness Avenue was the only way through the forest to Tower Road.

The "primitive road" description was accurate. I turned onto Wilderness Avenue and hesitated. A crude path disappeared into a tunnel of trees. I imagined it led to a dark world from which there was no return. Spring melt and recent rain created a muddy mess. What if I got stuck? Come on, I thought, people take trucks through stuff like this all the time. Commercials showed tough, mud-spattered trucks kicking ass in the wild. Fiona could do it. I flipped her into four-wheel drive and left behind the security of solid gravel. "Okay Fiona, get me to Tower Road."

At first, I steered her around the giant mud pits of unknown depth. Could those pits swallow us up whole? The road narrowed even more. We bounced and sloshed. Mud sprayed up and splattered the windshield as Fiona's front end plunged up and down. We were doing it. Just like the commercials. Until her tires sank deep into a pit. And stopped.

Shit. Were we stuck?

What if I had to spend the night out here? With no cell service, I'd have to walk for help. A long way for help. I'd be that person. I'd walk out of the forest and knock on a farmer's door. A matronly woman would answer. After hearing about my predicament, she'd shout over her shoulder, "Hey Howard, another idiot is stuck in the county forest!"

Determined not to be that idiot, I pressed the gas pedal. Fiona heaved, gaining only a few inches. My heart pounded.

SQUATTER

Beads of sweat burst out on my forehead. How could I be so stupid? My knuckles glared white as I gripped the steering wheel as if it were a weapon. I eased my foot on the pedal. "Come on…come on…COME ON!" I instinctively lifted my butt off the seat as if that would lighten Fiona's load, helping propel her forward. Fiona groaned and gave it her all. We inched forward and with a sudden jolt, broke free of the sucking mud. "Hey Hey!!" I yelled, which turned to laughing…that oh-my-gosh-I-got-myself-out-of-this-stupid-situation kind of laugh. I exhaled a long, heavy sigh of sweet relief.

The forest ahead brightened where the trees parted. That must be it. "WooHoo!" I yelled as I turned a mud splattered Fiona onto the solid gravel surface of Tower Road. We did it! I'm a badass now! Don't mess with me and muddy Fiona!

I drove north on Tower Road and pulled into the Timberland Wilderness trailhead parking. A mesh tent sat erected on the gravel. A young couple glanced at me from inside the tent. Okay. What's going on? I wondered. An afternoon rendezvous? I opened the truck door. Hordes of mosquitoes greeted me.

"Hello!" the woman said. "We haven't seen anyone all day."

"Are you guys okay?" I asked. There wasn't another vehicle in the rugged lot.

"Oh yeah, we're camping at Wood Lake," the man said. "We're from Iowa and thought we'd try hiking in northern Wisconsin, but we've never experienced mosquitoes like this before."

"We couldn't take it anymore," the woman continued. "We had to set up our tent for a break."

The tank shirts and shorts they wore certainly weren't appropriate for the thick bug conditions. People not familiar with Wisconsin's northwoods might not comprehend the bug situation. They look at you funny and their eyes narrow when you tell them that the mosquitoes are so thick they form clouds. If you stand still you can hear the forest humming with millions of mosquitoes. Their faces express obvious doubt. "Clouds? Really?" they ask with a hint of sarcasm. "A humming forest?" They don't believe you until they experience it for themselves.

I climbed into Fiona's bed to unload my bike for the short ride back down Tower Road to the other trailhead. "Would you like a ride to Wood Lake when I get back?" I offered. They declined and said they'd be okay after resting a while longer. I sped down Tower Road to outpace the militant mosquitoes on a mission of torture.

The other trailhead lacked a parking area. I dragged my bike through the soggy ditch and lugged it to the trail sign. The mosquitoes ambushed me, unphased by the spray I had recently doused myself with. My fingers fumbled with the lock while the pests swarmed my hands and face. They bit through the back of my shirt. "Screw it," I said and let my unlocked bike fall against the trail sign and ran into the woods followed by a posse of winged blood suckers.

Running–or my version of running which was a super-duper fast walk–proved the only way to stay relatively bug free. Even a quick stop to adjust my boot laces produced an immediate swarm. I ran past a bench that read, *Sit and Enjoy the Beauty of the Trail*. Stately trees rose from flooded areas behind the beaver dam making a portion of the woods look more like a Louisianan swamp than a Midwestern forest.

My bladder felt uncomfortably full. I couldn't pee back at the trailhead because the couple was there. There was no stopping now. If I dropped my pants my butt would become a mosquito pincushion in seconds. It would have to wait.

SQUATTER

    I burst out of the woods onto Tower Road. The couple was gone. Mosquitoes attacked Fiona's tires as I slipped off my pack, jumped into the front seat and slammed the door. I smashed the mosquitoes that followed me inside. After retrieving my bike, I cast aside all lady-likeness and peed right on the gravel road before heading home to Wausau.

    A burger sounded fantastic after dealing with all that mess. After weeks of closure, some restaurants reopened at 25% capacity. When cell service returned, I dialed Milwaukee Burger Company to see if they were open and had space. Something tickled my forehead. The phone rang. I swiped my forehead. It rang again. Something crawled along my hairline. I glanced in the rearview mirror. A black speck inched along above my glasses. A tick. I dropped my phone in my lap, rolled down the window and flicked the tick out onto the road. "Milwaukee Burger Company... hello?" echoed a cheery voice.

    Sitting at the bar in my campfire-smelling clothes and frazzled braids, I jotted down my hike's info in the Guidebook, while waiting on my longed-for burger. A guy sitting four empty stools away glanced at my book and asked, "Er ya hikin' dat whole trail?"

    Am I? Should I do the whole trail? My goal was the northern half. The four hundred-some miles from Wausau to the Wisconsin/Minnesota border. The part that I thought would be the best. That's presumptuous of me. How could I say one part was better if I didn't do it all? The whole thing huh?

    "Yeah. I am."

6

Mitch and I are entwined in some kind of twisted dance.

After returning from camping, I spent a day with Mitch. In bed. That was twice in a few weeks' time. I had been doing so well since February. Months had been wasted. The adventure in Death Valley, the yurt on Lake Superior, the Nebraska Sandhills road trip and camping at Rock Island ran like a movie reel through my mind. The exhilaration and giddy freedom from those experiences felt like they happened to someone else. Someone free, smart, and put together. I felt disgusted with myself. I wanted to fully let go. But couldn't. I also couldn't admit to others that I was still enmeshed in a destructive relationship. What moron continues seeing someone whose behavior is so appalling?

    I wouldn't be able to face questions such as: Why did you stay so long? Why didn't you break up earlier? Didn't you see the red flags? I wouldn't have had an answer. Because I didn't know why. To me, those questions held a hint of accusation that suggested it couldn't have been that bad. After all, if I'd chosen to stay, I'd chosen to play. That unspoken criticism added another ounce of shame on an already back-breaking load.

SQUATTER

* * *

There were clues in my childhood that my emotional well-being wasn't always great. I had an intense fear of death that resulted in screaming panic attacks. I didn't know anyone who had died. Just driving by a cemetery would set me off. But mostly, the panic would rise while lying in bed at night. I also suffered fierce stomachaches that drove me to curl up on my bed with my knees tucked underneath me and my face buried in my hands. I'd break out in a prickly sweat as I self-soothed by rocking back and forth.

I had everything that would indicate a good childhood. We had nice homes over the years, homemade meals, aesthetically beautiful holidays and piano lessons. But there was a lack of deep connection that I felt not only in our nuclear family but in our extended family as well.

In my teen years, I began unraveling. My relationship with food changed. I restricted calories and obsessed about my food intake. I didn't understand why or where that was coming from. It worried me, and I told a friend about it while on the phone. She went and got her mom, who told me I needed to tell my parents or she would. I told them, but don't remember much was done about it. I remember being at a doctor appointment. But otherwise, it really wasn't addressed. My recollection of our family life was that everyone should be happy and problems shouldn't exist. Thankfully, the food issue faded after leaving home.

I grew up voiceless and had no sense of self. The opinions of others easily swayed me since I had none of my own. The lack of agency left me behind my peers. At times, confusing anger overwhelmed me. I would be enraged over something like my hair not doing what I wanted it to do. I sometimes spewed meanness at my younger sister. One time, when I was in junior high, I said something about wanting her to get hit by a car. I wanted her to cry, so I could comfort her. How twisted was that? I didn't understand where that anger came from. I figured there had to be something wrong with me. But I didn't know what it could be.

My unraveling continued with a need for attention. Sometimes I went to a neighbor's house, feigning an illness or minor injury, with a strange desire for them to care for me. I spiraled through a promiscuous time, not only with peers but weeks after turning seventeen, I had slept with someone who was married.

While at a picnic table with my parents, alongside a Wisconsin River park, my newly eighteen-year-old self sat there as my mom pressed and pressed and pressed me for information about the troubles I had been having with my boyfriend. Conversations with my mom weren't an exchange of thoughts and ideas. She talked at me. She did monologues. I thought one-sided conversations were normal. I knew nothing else. After being pressed, I told her about the married guy I had seen a few times since turning seventeen. Her response was raging contempt. "I can't believe you would spread your legs like that," she hissed. My dad got up from the table, turned his back and walked away. I sat there. Stunned and silent. That's where that memory ends. I had checked out. While no parent would jump for joy at such behavior, I learned at that moment that no one would walk with me when I needed it most. Unbeknownst to me at the time, the Ice Age Trail sat yards away from that picnic table.

And then I left home. The rejection was more than I could take.

That defining moment as a teen encapsulated a childhood filled with shame that anchored itself deep in my soul, haunting me for decades. Childhood subconsciously taught me that shame was a normal part of love and relationships. I learned that the people who supposedly love you, shame you.

* * *

Mitch and I were entwined in some kind of twisted dance. Someone told me that dance was the abuse cycle. But no. It wasn't that. I would have seen that if it were true. The problem was me making stupid choices.

Again.

Because there was something wrong with me. Sure, Mitch was persistent, immature, and hadn't respected any boundary I'd set. He'd drop by, send cards, gifts and never-ending emails after I'd ask him to stop. But I didn't stand firm. I never learned how to create boundaries. Or even that I was allowed to. Did I even have boundaries? "What's wrong with you?" Mitch often asked in a sneering tone. That same question from my childhood followed me into my adulthood.

Mitch hadn't shown his ugly side recently. His emails gushed with love, but rage brewed under the surface when we were together. He'd swallow hard and blink when I mentioned my travels and adventures. He held his tongue in order to win me back into full relationship status. That would never happen. But we were still bonded together and no matter what I tried, I couldn't let go.

* * *

An eighteen-mile road walk near my home led south to the county line. The day after seeing Mitch, I began chipping away at it. Because that trail stretch was nearby, I bike shuttled and walked it over multiple days. One of the days I stopped at a country bar for a bite to eat. Rural bars would be an interesting way to experience an area's local culture, so why not try one in my home county.

The bar sat back from the road surrounded by a gravel lot. An oasis in a county mixed with woods and farm fields. Marathon County wasn't quite "Up North" where lush, national forests drew outdoor enthusiasts. And it wasn't south enough, near the state's larger cities, where better economic opportunity helped to maintain charming, manicured farms that could be featured on a magazine cover, stirring up dreams of country living. Instead, Marathon County was a gas stop on the way "Up North," dotted with tired, worn-out dairy farms trying to scratch out a living while competing with monstrous milking operations.

As I approached the bar's entrance, multiple ATVs sat out front. A couple of stout women with harsh blonde hair stood near the door holding cigarettes. Ribbons of smoke rose into the air. They reminded me of the kind of girls who were feared in high school because of their propensity for fighting. Their mid-1980s hairstyles and black eyeliner aided in the revival of that memory. I smiled and nodded to them, subtly holding my breath while passing through the cloud of smoke. They did not return my gesture.

Slipping off my daypack, I took a seat at the bar and looked forward to something yummy. The bartender stood a few feet away, talking with other customers. He wasn't exactly talking, but ranting…about masks. "If anyone dares come in here wearin' a mask…!" Masks were only suggested at that time, not required. I was not wearing one. I sat and waited. I glanced at the ranting bartender. He glanced at me. I swiped through Facebook. I feigned interest in the overhead TV. After running out of pretend stuff to occupy the time, I nonchalantly walked to the bathroom and returned. Awkward minutes passed.

Other than the two people listening to his ranting, it was just me sitting at the bar. Yet, he wouldn't acknowledge me. Was there something weird about me? I wasn't wearing anything that made a statement about a political party, school or another state that might have offended him. The only thing that stood out was that I was a woman alone and obviously a hiker in a room of ATVers. It was time to leave. For whatever reason, he wasn't going to serve me. I picked up my pack and walked out like it was no big deal. My first rural bar experience on the trail.

* * *

Nearly a month had passed since Anna dropped me off at the Plover River trailhead for the twenty-four-mile day. I finished my home county, along with miles in the neighboring ones. After recent heavy rains, I returned north, eager to complete my second county.

I rounded a curve on remote Conservation Road and slammed on the brakes. Fiona skidded to a stop on the wet gravel, in front of a gaping hole. The previous night's pounding rain had washed out the road, exposing the metal culvert that had failed to contain the storm's torrent. If I had been going any faster, Fiona would have nosedived. After backing up from the chasm, I stepped out and gawked at the damage. Damn. The forest stood peaceful as morning sunbeams threaded through the trees like party streamers. But hours ago, raging water had pushed through those woods, taking the road with it. I needed a new plan. Unfortunately, Conservation Road didn't go all the way through to Tower Road. Tower Road was becoming a thorn in my side.

Determined to finish my second county, I studied the map for directions to Tower Road. Again. Last time, Wilderness Road delivered me through. But that was coming from west of Tower. I was on the east side and according to the map there was no access. That meant miles of extra driving down Highway E and west on Highway M until it met Tower Road. Then more miles north on Tower to the trailhead. Basically, a big square that would cost me time. When cell service returned on the drive, I called the sheriff's department to report the road wash out.

After the long detour to Tower Road and a packed lunch, it was one o'clock. It would stay light until after seven. I tossed a head lamp into my pack, doused myself with bug spray and entered the Camp 27 segment, named after one of the many logging camps that once dotted the northern forests.

Mosquitoes buzzed around my ears and in my face. After swatting for the eleven hundredth time, I pulled on my head net, which I had hoped to avoid after spending all my time at work wearing a mask and face shield. I had recently heard of permethrin in a Facebook group. It was a kind of insect repellent treatment for clothes that lasted through many washings. But I'd been too focused on getting out on the trail and the mess with Mitch that I didn't take the time to figure it out.

The forest hummed again from the droning of mosquitoes. What if I collapsed out here from a stroke and thousands of mosquitoes feasted on me? Could someone die from that?

I spent the afternoon battling water and mud that spanned the forest floor as far as I could see. I didn't have daylight to waste putzing around balancing on logs or hopping on random dry spots. So, I walked the miles in ankle and calf deep mud. Goop gripped my boots, reluctantly releasing its hold with a sucking noise as it yielded to my momentum.

My Crocs dangled from my pack, but I couldn't stop to change or I'd be overcome by mosquitoes. I couldn't run like I did on Timberland Wilderness because the mud and water hid rocks and other obstacles. The idea of getting injured and forced to stop made me shudder.

I sloshed from yellow blaze to yellow blaze on the invisible trail. The dense forest canopy blocked out the blue sky and sunshine. Over three hours later, sunlight shone through where the trees parted. Conservation Road. In the open sun, the mosquitoes became manageable. With relief, I dropped my pack on the road, stripped off my socks and boots and laid them on the gravel to dry in the sunshine. I unwrapped a fig bar, dug out my paper map and planned my next step.

I was basically trapped. Conservation Road dead-ended to the west and was washed out to the east. No cell service. Even if I could call someone, they wouldn't get past the wash out. I began to think that hiking here today hadn't been the wisest choice. Oddly enough, I wasn't nervous. Even though I was surrounded by miles of dense forest, being near my home territory gave me comfort. The Great Unknown from my youth was vast and wild, but it wasn't too far from my own backyard.

The late afternoon shadows stretched across the road. It had taken me over three hours to get here. Should I backtrack the way I came? I squinched my nose at the thought of another three hours plodding through mud and battling bugs. I studied the map. I could walk Conservation Road toward its dead end and hope to pick the right logging road that would connect to the trail. From there it would only be a few trail miles to where Fiona sat waiting. According to the guidebook, which I left behind with Fiona, I recalled that a logging road met the trail from Conservation Road. But what if it didn't? Or what if I walked the wrong logging road and missed the entry to the trail?

It was 4:45 pm and I needed to make a decision. Staying on gravel would be easier, therefore, I chose to walk to the end of the road, knowing there was no turning back or I could get stuck out there in the dark. I changed into a new pair of socks, tucked my pants legs into them for tick protection and wore my Crocs. Dry socks felt good. After a few minutes of walking, my ankles began to itch. I ignored it and kept moving. But then they were really itching. I looked down at my feet. Dozens of mosquitoes covered my ankles. I forgot to spray my new socks.

I reached for the side of my pack to grab my can of bug spray. It wasn't there. I slipped off my pack and searched it. Nothing. Maybe it rolled out of my pack and into the grass while I took a break on the road. I had to go back to check. It wasn't far. I ran back and searched but didn't find it. I remembered bending over while on the trail to quickly re-tie one of my boots. The can must have slipped out of its mesh pouch. Fuck.

Now I really couldn't get stuck out here all night without bug spray, I thought, and cringed at the idea of trying to protect myself from mosquitoes. I pulled on the previously sprayed wet socks over the dry ones and headed back down Conservation Road. The late day sun urged me on. The wet socks remained mosquito free.

I came to a fork in the road that wasn't on my printed map. I couldn't recall if the road forked on the guidebook map. Shit. Right went slightly north. Left stayed west. I chose left, only because it didn't change direction. If all else failed, when Conservation Road ended, I could bushwhack west through the woods until it took me to Tower Road.

After I walked for an hour, the road ended at a dark forest wall. A speck of something looked odd against the white bark of a tree. "Please be what I think it is," I mumbled. A small, square, brown sign with a yellow arrow pointing south was nailed to a birch tree. It pointed toward an overgrown logging road. I sighed in giddy relief. The logging road brought me to the division of Camp 27 and Newwood segments. That meant I had to re-hike three muddy miles of Camp 27. But I didn't care. I would have crawled through the mud just to know that I was on the right trail back to Fiona.

I emerged from the woods onto Tower Road and smiled at the sight of Fiona. Over thirteen muddy miles in six hours with an hour of daylight to spare. I hopped into Fiona and bounced along to my cranked-up playlist as I headed home to Wausau. Not only had I completed my second county that day, I'd faced down a road washout, change of plans, lots of uncertainty…all in a remote area. All with no cell service. All on my own.

I so got this, I thought.

After arriving home, I opened my spam folder. Mitch had sent twenty-two emails in the last twelve hours.

7

I think I'm addicted to Mitch.

I hadn't explored Langlade County, my neighbor to the northeast, so it was a bit of a mystery to me. Just over 19,000 people lived within its 888 square-mile borders. My only experience with the county was that my late husband had leased his semi to a trucking company in the small town of Antigo. I'd driven there a number of times over the years on two-lane roads, through dense woods. Weary-looking homes reflected the fact that twenty percent of the county's children lived in poverty.

I studied the trail map and decided to complete Langlade's segments in order. That meant first tackling a twenty-four-mile road walk. Dividing it into two days would have done it. "Nah, just get 'er done in one day," I told myself. It would be the longest distance I'd ever walked in a day—a half-mile longer than the Marathon County Day on April 30.

I certainly didn't want to bike *and* walk twenty-four miles. My daughter, Liz, was the answer. On a mid-June morning, I bought her coffee and a donut, and we left Fiona at the county line trailhead as the sun rose. Liz dropped me off on a remote road.

I focused on my rhythmic plodding as the road stretched before me and the miles passed. Initially, I followed the suggested route. A yellowish, 1970s pickup truck rumbled up next to me, dramatically sagging sideways. "Ice Age Trail?" a gray-bearded man wearing a plaid shirt asked. His arm casually rested on the open window. He never came to a full stop. "Yep! Thanks for checking!" I replied. With a nod and a wave he drove off. Other than curious cows, he was the only contact I had with another living being all morning.

By 11:30, I had walked nine miles and felt pretty good. I'm gonna rock this day, I smiled to myself. A countryside church came into view. A perfect lunch stop. I filled my 2.5-liter bladder and a water bottle before leaving that morning, but as the day grew warm, my water lessened. There had to be a spigot outside the church. I spied a pickup truck parked next to the entrance of St. Peter Lutheran Church. I approached a man who was loading shovels into the truck's bed and asked him about a spigot.

"Are you walking a long way?" the man asked after greeting me good morning.

"I'm doing a twenty-four-mile day on one of the Ice Age Trail road walks," I said. He smiled as he pulled out keys from his jeans pocket and unlocked the church doors.

"Help yourself to the bathroom, and there's a water fountain in the hallway."

I couldn't turn down an offer for the bathroom. I had already taken multiple lightning-fast potty breaks at the side of the road. I welcomed toilet paper and soap. A couple of years earlier, before I purchased reusable pee cloths, I learned a hard lesson about peeing in the woods and wiping with leaves.

I knew about poison ivy–leaves of three, let them be. But apparently, I didn't know about poison oak. Mitch and I had been hiking and I did my business in the woods. A couple of days later, my nether regions were ON FIRE. I sent Mitch running to the store for itch relief spray while I lay groaning and holding a bag of frozen peas between my legs. He returned and fumbled about, unsure of what to do. I laid back, spread my legs and wailed, "Just spray it on!" Steroid cream eventually did the trick, and I was left with a story about dumb things you shouldn't do while in the woods.

I thanked the man for letting me use the facilities and ate my sandwich on a shaded picnic table behind the church. Sixteen miles to go. The blazing noon sun had stolen the low morning light that created long, cool shadows across the road. I reapplied sunscreen. My shoulders turned pink underneath my long-sleeved shirt. Redheads and sunshine are always at war. I made a mental note to look into buying a UV protectant shirt.

My legs and hips ached. It wasn't my muscles that hurt. Deep, throbbing bone pain usually began about the eight-mile mark of a hike. I found momentary relief by squatting. That position squeezed the pain away–a hurt-so-good kind of feeling. My fingers ballooned up into sausage-like digits. I held up my hands in a surrendering-to-the-police position as I walked to relieve the swelling.

The sun beat down on my pack, turning my water unpleasantly warm. I craved a cool drink. I veered off the suggested route in order to pass a large cemetery. Cemeteries generally have nice lawns. And nice lawns need water. My hunch was correct, and I filled up on one of the many spigots at Elmwood Cemetery on the outskirts of Antigo.

I checked my phone. It was just after two. The afternoon dragged on. A greasy mix of sweat and sunscreen dripped down my face. Because of the reroute past the cemetery, I would have to walk a short distance on busy Highway 45.

SQUATTER

Past a gas station. I daydreamed about the wonderful things found at gas stations. Cold things. I could be there in less than an hour. Walk. Squat. Raise hands. Dream about cold things.

The gas station was just ahead, and I moved toward it like a parched, desert traveler staggering to an oasis. I marched straight to the bathroom. Standing on the chipped, worn floor tiles that looked like they were from the 1930s, I spun the metal faucet handle and cupped my hands under the cool water to rinse away the slime on my face. My whole body hurt. I stiffly wandered the narrow aisles and grabbed a Gatorade and a Snickers ice cream bar. It didn't occur to me to purchase pain reliever. I rarely ever used them other than for an occasional headache. Not being an athlete, I never experienced that level of body pain.

A bubbly young woman greeted me from behind the counter. "Did ya walk here?" she asked, glancing at my backpack while scanning my purchases. "I did!" I said, and told her that I was section-hiking the Ice Age Trail.

"Never heard of it…but that's so cool though…like…ya know…to do somethin' big like that," she said with gusto. I was doing something big. Sometimes a stranger can give you the lift you need.

With my icy-cold treasures in hand, I waddled toward the one table wedged between automotive accessories and the window, easing into the chair with sweet relief. I guzzled my Gatorade. A coffee pot and a popcorn maker stood in the corner. I imagined local old timers gathering for coffee every morning while contemplating all the wrongs in the world.

Bubbly Girl leaned over the counter on her elbows and continued chatting with me while I devoured my ice cream bar. I learned that she was in a bowling league and had a boyfriend. "I wanna do somethin' big too. I never been outta Wisconsin…well…we camped in the UP once…and that was like…real cool…but that's it. I never even seen Madison…someday I'll leave this place." She had big dreams like many young people do. Strangely, I don't remember having any as a young adult. Dreaming big requires belief in yourself. You have to believe you're worthy of dreams before you can have them.

My body had become rigid in that short time of sitting. It took a few waddling steps to loosen up. I said goodbye to Bubbly Girl with Big Dreams and wished her well. I had seven miles to go.

It took me three hours to walk those last seven miles. Not because of hills or other obstacles. I simply had a hard time moving. After lots of groans, agony relieving squats, heavy exhales and cursing, one mile remained. I plopped down onto the side of the road. I couldn't go anymore. Not even another mile. I Facetimed my daughter, Grace. "Whatcha doin?" She answered in typical teen fashion.

"Nuthin."

"I can't go anymore, Grace," I whined. "Just talk to me, k?"

"About what?"

"Anything. Tell me about One Direction. Tell me how cute Harry Styles is."

I forced myself to stand up. Grace's voice encouraged me forward.

"Well, 'Watermelon Sugar' is newer…" Ahh yes, that song that always seemed to be playing on the radio when I turned on the truck.

"Oh… and I watched Dunkirk again today…" A great way to get kids interested in a historical movie was to cast one of the most popular boy-band singers of all time.

SQUATTER

I walked with a gait that was well beyond my fifty-two years. By the time Fiona came into view, I was a full-fledged member of the Harry Styles Fan Club. After eleven hours of walking, I collapsed in Fiona's front seat. I called Sam's Pizza for an order to go. Forty minutes later I limped out of the pizza shop with my delicious reward.

* * *

After a recovery day, it was time to do actual Langlade County trail miles. Much of the trail winds through the county forest making bike shuttling long and laborious due to few roads. Once again, Liz was my shuttle ride. We rose before dawn and stopped at Kwik Trip for a coffee and donut bribe for Liz.

I had heard in the Facebook group that it was easy to get lost in the nearly ten-mile Kettlebowl segment. The trail through Langlade County had a reputation for being overgrown, which often obscured the already sparsely marked blazes. The trail depended on volunteers for maintenance. In a low-population county where ATVing reigns, it was no easy task to find volunteers interested in hiking culture.

The Kettlebowl segment was named for the frost pockets found in the area. Frost pockets are grassy depressions in the forest with steep sides formed by ice chunks that broke free from the glacial ice sheet. Imagine a kettle set in the ground, thus the name Kettlebowl. Just as mountains have timber lines where trees no longer grow, frost pockets or kettles also have one, except it is reversed. Cooler, heavier air settles in the pocket preventing larger vegetation growth.

We left Fiona at a rural cemetery near the southern Kettlebowl trailhead, and Liz dropped me off at the other end. I wore a whistle around my neck, a bear bell clipped to one of my boots, bear spray on my belt and carried a rain jacket in my pack. I didn't fear contact with bears. They wanted to avoid me as much as I wanted to avoid them. But there was the possibility of accidentally coming between a mama bear and her cubs. That wouldn't be good. Mama bears don't like that. I wanted something other than my bare hands to protect myself from any possibility: roaming dogs, humans up to no good…anything.

The trail was indeed overgrown and sparsely marked. I stopped where logging roads intersected to scan the area for trail markings. I slopped through muddy messes and high wet grass, but to my pleasant surprise the morning was nearly mosquito free. Since the bugs were at bay, I decided to bop down a short spur trail to Kent Hill, the highest point in Langlade County. I envisioned eating lunch with a view of the surrounding forest, but thick foliage obstructed the scene. Maybe I wasn't in the right spot. But I didn't want to stray far from the spur trail and get lost.

Erratics dotted the forest floor. The boulders had been transported and left behind long ago by glacial ice. I perched myself on one to eat lunch. The trail wasn't well used. It was plausible that I might be the first human to ever touch that rock. It had been there centuries before I was born and would be there centuries after I'm gone.

While eating, I reflected on what a friend said last year about being addicted to Mitch. She said it is hard to leave "those kinds of relationships." I wasn't exactly sure what that meant. I wondered if I might be in one of those kinds of relationships. For the first time, I acknowledged that I had an addiction to Mitch. I didn't know how it happened or what I was going to do about it, but it was true. Thunder rumbled in the distance. I put on my rain jacket and finished Kettlebowl in a downpour.

SQUATTER

* * *

I took a three-week break from the trail to help my son John and his wife move to Texas, after his military stint ended. They had a baby and a two-year-old, doubling my number of grandchildren since meeting Mitch. Before leaving, I learned about an app called Guthook-—a GPS tracking app for hikers and purchased it. In the busyness of those weeks, I promptly forgot about it (The app is currently called FarOut, but I will refer to it by the name it was at the time).

Mitch's daily messages continued to pour in. We went round and round, like always. *That is the stupidest thing I ever heard come out of your brain*, he wrote in response to my attempts to express myself. I knew he would never hear me. But strangely, I kept trying.

I returned to the trail in mid-July. Liz and I did our early morning Kwik Trip stop and returned to Langlade County. We parked Fiona and drove to where the trail exited on County Highway A. The guidebook said there would be no parking. Our plan was that I would hop out of the car and be on my way. Our plan failed when we couldn't find the trailhead. Inching along Highway A, we scanned the treeline for the familiar brown and yellow Ice Age Trail sign. Nothing. We turned around. Again, nothing.

"We've passed it! Turn around again," I said, my frustration brewing.

Liz, with more patience and grace at her age than I'd ever possess, turned the car around once again without a flicker of irritation. We couldn't find the sign.

"We need to flip the plan," I said with exasperation.

"Maybe try another day," Liz said in her gentle manner.

"I don't wanna waste a day, we've already driven out here. The trail is here."

We retrieved Fiona twenty minutes away and returned to park her along Highway A. But where? A sign for Peters Marsh State Wildlife Area seemed near to where the trail should emerge. I would walk to the wildlife area after finishing the segment.

After all that fuss, I finally hit the trail two hours after my planned start time. My irritation melted away after entering the sanctuary of the forest. I soon arrived at the site of the Norem Lumber Camp. Disintegrating foundations and an old root cellar, nicknamed the Hillbilly Hilton, were all that remained of the early twentieth-century camp. I opened the cellar's wooden door at the side of a grassy mound and stepped inside. The stale air hung thick and musty. Two wooden bunks and basic cookware were available for those who wished to use the root cellar for shelter. I imagined the cellar as a childhood paradise in which to pass summer afternoons playing "olden days", pretending to be Laura Ingalls living in a prairie dugout.

Hours later, I pushed through a sea of waist-high ferns from one blaze to the next. I followed the foliage's slightest indentation indicating another person had come through---almost as though a pizza cutter had sliced through the vegetation leaving a razor-thin line. After twelve miles of traversing overgrown, muddy forest, I staggered out onto Highway A. Liz and I had driven past that spot multiple times, but foliage concealed the sign. I walked toward Peters Marsh. Wasn't the sign just around the bend? It seemed closer when we were driving. I fumed and my jaw tightened. "Gosh dang it all, where is that frickin' sign?" I pulled out my phone to check Google Maps for the exact distance, but it wouldn't load. A fleeting temptation to flag down a car and ask for a ride crossed my mind. But I kept walking.

SQUATTER

After a half a mile of fuming, the Peters Marsh sign came into view. I'd had enough frustration for one day. After returning home, the memory of purchasing the Guthook app before the Texas trip popped into my head. The GPS would have enabled us to see our location in relation to the trail. The Highway A trailhead would have been easy to find as well as the trail's distance to Peters Marsh. My foolish blunder cost us time and needless frustration. I omitted that part of the story in my Facebook update in the Ice Age Trail group. No need to reveal that an incompetent idiot was on the trail.

* * *

More heavy rains soaked the area. I needed a break from the endless mud of Langlade County's logging roads. I headed one county south to give Langlade time to dry out.

During a road walk, a man with a slight build wearing a backpack and carrying a walking stick approached me from the other direction. He had to be a hiker. Funny how the first person I'd encounter on the trail wasn't on the actual trail. The wiry, energetic man, who appeared to be well into his retirement years, greeted me with a pleasant smile.

"Another hiker!" he said. "I never see anyone."

"Me neither! You're the first person I've run into," I said, glancing at his ornate walking stick.

"I'm Lyle, but you can call me Lit'le Bit," he said, and spelled it out.

"Lit'le Bit?" I repeated.

"Yep, my trail name, as in let's go just a little bit more." Lit'le Bit had hiked the Appalachian Trail over the course of eight summers. "I always tried to get my hiking buddies to go just a little bit more before stopping for the day…

so that's what they named me. I got this walking stick out there, too." He held it out.

"Wow, it's beautiful," I said, admiring the mountain scene carved into the wood.

"What's your trail name?" he asked.

"Well…I hike solo, so I don't have one. I guess I'm just Yolanda," I said feeling a bit disappointed. Having a trail name sounded cool.

"Maybe you'll get one…you've got lots of miles yet," he said.

Lit'le Bit had retired from teaching and was section-hiking the Ice Age Trail at his leisure. "I can hike anytime I want…oh…and my wife is keeping an online journal of my hikes." He mentioned its web address, which I repeated several times so as not to forget. We talked more about the trail before parting ways. He took off down the road at an impressive speed. I continued on in my direction and found myself walking in step to the rhythmic clicking of his stick on the blacktop until the sound faded into the cornfields lining the road. Inspired by Lit'le Bit's energy, I envisioned a positive future regarding physical activity and aging.

That was July 30. I passed the two-hundred-mile mark. Against my better judgment, I spent the next day with Mitch.

"Hey," he said, and greeted me with a deep kiss when I arrived.

Last fall, I agreed to keep the physical part of our relationship going. Why not keep the one good thing we had?

But now as we embraced, I felt detached. His familiar hands glided over my skin. Something was different. I was different. I don't know if I want to keep doing this, I thought while glancing around the chaotic home of the man I knew wasn't capable of healthy love. The mental fog that had shrouded my vision for nearly three years was a little less dense, helping me to see that I, too, needed to learn the dynamics of healthy love.

My head rested on his chest. I listened to the relaxed breathing of the man I almost married and thought, this can't go on, but am I strong enough to let go? I left knowing that the answer to letting go of Mitch would be found on the trail. The more days I spent walking in solitude, the clearer this became.

* * *

I returned to my nemesis, Langlade County. It had to be done. The mud battle continued. I pushed through the jungle of ferns and mystery plants that came up to the armpits of my 5'8" frame. Guthook became my friend, helping me spot concealed trail markings.

At Game Lake, under a canopy of giant pines, the forest floor was dry and fairly clear of vegetation. Less vegetation meant fewer mosquitoes. I hadn't seen another person on any of the Langlade County trails. I stripped off my clothes, hung them on a branch and slipped into the cool water of Game Lake. There's something primal about being naked in the wilderness. Being vulnerable to the elements. Nothing separates you from the natural world. Water glided over every inch of my skin, adorning me in nature's finest silk. The cool, northern lake left me feeling invigorated and alive. I stepped onto the shore and dried in the summer sun before dressing. The fresh feeling of nature's kiss remained on my skin as I continued down the trail.

Later that day, I stopped at a warming house where the trail met up with ski trails. I dug out a snack from my pack and began reading the house's logbook.

February 9…a white/gray long-haired wild human was dismembering a rabbit…we immediately hid behind the door… there was scratching and digging outside.

I love a good imagination…

I am recording the events of March 9…In them-thar hills lurks a creature of immense size and ferocity looking to drag away any unsuspecting sojourner lacking the appropriate Yeti whistle…I was able to outdistance the horrible creature but not without suffering severe emotional trauma.

Who's to say there aren't creatures we haven't discovered yet living in the woods?

Things aren't always what they seem…strange beings lurk around northern Wisconsin.

While those accounts may be the product of creative imaginations and local brew, stories of creatures roaming northern Wisconsin have been around a long time. In the 1800s, newspapers reported that a creature terrorized the northern forests. The Hodag, a lizard-like beast with spikes down its back, was the talk of area lumber camps. Tales of the creature may have originated from Native American stories of water panthers and spirit beings. In 1893, Gene Shepard, a respected land surveyor and timber cruiser, claimed he captured a live Hodag. After keeping it in his barn, he showed it at the 1896 Oneida County Fair. Only the bravest of souls paid a nickel to witness the monster for themselves. Shepard later admitted that the beast was a wood carving covered in ox hide. What a shyster, I thought. I guess they've always been around.

What if the logbook writers saw Bigfoot? According to the Bigfoot Field Researchers Organization (BFRO), nearly one hundred Bigfoot sightings had been reported in Wisconsin since the 1970s. Many of those sightings were credible enough that in 2016, TV's Animal Planet sent a team to northern Wisconsin to film an episode of Finding Bigfoot. Three of those one hundred sightings were in Langlade County, with the most recent being January 2016. The BFRO classified that sighting as a Class A, meaning the possibility of misinterpretation of what the viewer saw was very low. Basically, they concluded Bigfoot had been seen in Langlade County.

    I wondered where I could buy a Yeti whistle.

8

I've had enough of his verbal vomit.

My fiercely independent nature wanted to do the trail solo. But there was value in meeting people with shared interests. I had made a slow exit from my social group after the 2016 election. The trail could bring new friends. It would be easy to social-distance while outside. In the trail's Facebook group, I responded to a post from Laura, looking for a hiking partner for a couple of days. She looked to be near my age. A safe bet. Someone easy to keep up with.

We planned to spend a few early August days checking off segments in the northwestern part of the state. We had permission to camp on lakeside private property belonging to a trail volunteer. I followed her directions and drove down a grassy path through the woods. I stopped at a narrow bridge spanning a creek-- not more than a few feet wide. There's no way that's gonna support Fiona, I thought. It looked like a bridge for little forest gnomes. But Laura said the owner claimed it was safe for a truck. A Tonka truck maybe. I held my breath and clenched the steering wheel as Fiona rolled across. The path soon opened up to a pristine lake. We were welcome to camp at the lakeside, enjoy the dock, and use the water bikes.

Laura was from the Madison area and had begun hiking the trail the previous December. Because she worked for

SQUATTER

the school system, she was able to put in serious miles over the summer.

"You're comfortable sleeping in that little car?" I asked when she showed me blankets laid across the backseat. I towered over her and imagined that she probably fit quite well.

"Oh yeah, I've been out for two weeks this stretch," she said.

We continued chatting as I opened Fiona's tailgate to retrieve camping chairs.

"Ack!" I yelled, startled by the unexpected movement of a mouse darting out from Fiona's bed. It scampered with lightning speed, disappearing behind the bumper.

Before leaving home, I loaded a cardboard box from the garage that was filled with old newspapers and kindling. The mouse must have been in the box. I opened the camping chairs and saw that the mouse had chewed a hole through one of them. Thank goodness I kept my $400 ultralight tent in the backseat and not in the bed.

After setting up the chairs, I hopped on one of the water bikes while Laura watched from the sandy shore. As I pedaled past the dock, pain pierced my arm.

"Ack!!" I shrieked once again. What the fuck was that? A giant, ugly wasp, with dangling long legs, flew past me. I winced and rubbed my arm to soothe the sting.

Laura jumped to my attention once again-- my second distress call in less than fifteen minutes. "Are you okay?" She had to think I was a nutcase. Concerned about the possibility of a reaction, since I'd always been plagued with allergies and breathing problems, I rinsed my arm with cool lake water and took a Benadryl.

After the excitement of the mouse and wasp drama died down, Laura chatted away about the trail. With exuberance, she told me about the counties and segments that were in my future.

"When you get to that bend in the road in Waushara County…oh, the water can be deep on the Storr's Lake segment…make sure you stop and eat at…" She was a walking trail encyclopedia.

"Do you have a trail name yet?" I asked her, thinking about Lit'le Bit.

"Energizer Bunny in Human Form," she said. "Energizer for short."

"Oh. Cool." Well, that killed my hopes that she'd be someone easy to keep up with.

Laura never tired or showed signs of slowing down during the fifteen miles of our first day. She scurried up hills and patiently waited as I inched my way up. Her firecracker energy couldn't be due to youthfulness because she was only six years younger than me. After hours of my arms swinging at my sides, my hands swelled up again, looking like thick man hands.

"You need hiking poles," Laura said matter-of-factly. Mitch had them for us in Hawaii and Arizona, so I assumed poles were for mountain terrain. "Poles allow your upper body to take on some of the work in propelling yourself forward…it's way easier to tackle long mileage days. They also keep your hands from swelling."

I was sold and planned to order a pair.

We drove to another county and shared a ten-dollar campsite along the Yellow River in the town of Gilman, population 390.

"The pit toilets are open," I said. That was a pleasant surprise, since many park facilities were locked during Covid. Both evenings, I stripped down to my underwear and dipped in the river before making a campfire for us. Laura retired each night to her car. I stayed in my tent. Trains roared throughout the two nights on nearby tracks, shaking the ground beneath me. Their rumbling eventually stopped waking me and the commotion became a part of my dreams.

Our last day together was a fourteen-mile road walk that would take us from the edge of the Chequamegon National Forest to the Taylor/Chippewa County line. At mid-morning, we were greeted by a festive, white-washed sign that read, Hello! God Bless America, Welcome to Lublin. Early settlers named the town after Lublin, Poland.

We explored the grounds of a church and cemetery that had Eastern European roots. The church's cross had three bars, with the bottom one being slanted. I later learned that Orthodox churches used the "Eastern Cross" tradition. The upper bar represented the sign that hung above Jesus saying that he was King of the Jews and the lower, slanted bar was where his feet were nailed.

The road led to the heart of the village with a population of 108. A man in faded jeans and a checkered shirt crossed the street up ahead, passing a weather-worn building that leaned so severely it was propped up by a large beam.

"Good morning!" Laura called out and waved. Her energizer-energy not only applied to her physical attributes but also to her eagerness to reel in anyone within shouting distance for a conversation. The man smiled and changed direction, walking toward us. He stopped at a socially acceptable distance. Gray hair poked out from underneath a frayed baseball cap that advertised Kolve's Corner Bar. I looked past him and caught sight of a bar bearing the same name.

"Hi ladies, 'name's Richard," he said. "You both look new to town...hiking the trail I take it?" We confirmed, introduced ourselves and asked him about the church we passed at the edge of town.

"That's the Holy Assumption Orthodox Church...one of the last continuously running orthodox churches in Wisconsin. It's well over a hundred years old," he said in a way that made me think he'd recited the information before. He talked about the community as if he was promoting it.

Then, with a big grin, he changed the topic. "I'm running for State Assembly!" He unbuttoned his checkered shirt to reveal a green t-shirt promoting his campaign. "I hope to represent my district even though I've only been here thirty years." Generational longevity means something in rural communities. We chatted about his campaign and how he hoped to win against a candidate who had been serving for many years.

"Well, good luck to you," Laura said as we prepared to walk on.

"Yes, good luck, nice to meet you," I said, and reached out to shake his hand. He didn't take it. I immediately cringed, at my foolish gesture. Oh my gosh. It's Covid, you idiot, I thought. No one shakes hands anymore. I'd spent so much time alone on the trail that sometimes Covid didn't seem real. The trail made it easy to leave reality behind.

Walking through the rest of Lublin, we passed the remnants of a '76 gas station. Rusty trucks from another era sat engulfed in the high grass--their final resting place after a prime life that occurred well before Richard's arrival to the area.

SQUATTER

Road walks inevitably pass country churches, indicating that the roots of faith run deep in rural America. Laura and I passed signs mounted on mailbox posts bearing scripture. *Salvation is found nowhere else, for there is no other name under heaven by which we must be saved. Acts 4:12.* One sign wasn't a verse but read, *God knows your thoughts.* I pondered the intention of the sign owner. Was it to instill fear? Was it to offer comfort? Either way, if God knew my thoughts, then at least someone did, because I found my thoughts about Mitch confusing.

    I was elated at the sight of Fiona waiting for us at the Otter Lake Bait Shop at the county line on Highway H. Fighting against my body stiffness and pain. I attempted to walk into the store like a normal human being. Laura seemed unphased by the fourteen-mile road walk and entered the shop as spritely as ever. She was one of those people who could crank out a twenty-mile day like it was nothing. I practically died on the two, twenty-plus mile days I had done. She reigned in the clerk. "So, Tiffany…" Laura had learned her name and chatted away. I slunk through the store, keeping my bodily misery to myself. My stiff bones throbbed. I wanted to fold them up and squeeze out the pain. Laura joined me in looking for treats. "Feeling okay?" she asked.

    "The same as always on these long days," I said. I wanted to say freaking horrible, but that would make me a complete downer.

    We were more than happy to spend money at the shop after they allowed us to park Fiona there all day. We picked out soda and ice cream and gaped at the frozen pizzas.

"I'd be happy to heat up a pizza for you," Tiffany said, noticing our desiring gaze. Laura's talent for making instant friends paid off for us at that moment.

We took off our packs at the one table in the store and sat down surrounded by items that made the rural shop a necessity for those coming to fish at nearby Otter Lake. A refrigerator containing bait stood next to the table. Thirty worms for $3.75. Crawlers could be bought by the dozen in regular or jumbo size. Jars of pickled green beans, peppers, asparagus, and beets lined a pine board shelf. Most likely, generations of experience went into those jars. Mounted fish, deer, and even a bear looked down upon us from the walls.

"When you get down to my area in Dane County, you can stay in my guest room if Covid is better by then. Or you can camp in my yard," Laura offered. I accepted her yard offer. Even if the Covid numbers improved, the darned asthma I suffered from cats, which Laura had, would keep me from enjoying her guest room.

Tiffany brought us our pizza, and we devoured it.

* * *

In late August, I took a week's break from the trail and made it to Isle Royale. Alone. Almost a year had passed since my trip to Rock Island, when a solo trip to Isle Royale was unattainable for me. But a spark smoldered throughout the last year, waiting to flare up at the right time.

I'd built my confidence while traveling, camping, and hiking the trail; I was ready for Isle Royale. Being the year of Covid, the ferries to the island weren't running. If you didn't own your own boat, the only way to Isle Royale was by seaplane.

I sat, wearing a mask, next to the pilot and stuffed in the squishy ear plugs I was given. The plane roared down the Keweenaw Waterway in Hancock, Michigan. Water thrusted up alongside the plane. We soared over Lake Superior. I gazed at the gentle curve of the water's horizon. Mitch and I had always taken the ferry because he brought along his canoe. I savored that the seaplane experience would be mine, alone, one untarnished by ugliness.

We landed in Windigo, the opposite end of the island from where Mitch and I explored. I was one of the lucky few who made it to Isle Royale during the 2020 season. I wouldn't backpack impressive miles or traverse the length of the island. I just wanted to make it to paradise myself. Within minutes of my hike, I passed a moose with her calf feeding in a creek. My welcome-to-the-island gift.

I backpacked the six miles to Huginnin Cove in complete misery, certain the thirty-eight-pound pack on my 128 pound frame would kill me before I got to the cove. My head throbbed. The waist belt cinched my gut and pressed on my bony hips. Canoeing with Mitch had been much easier. Ideally, a backpack shouldn't weigh more than 20% of a person's body weight. Mine was almost 30%. But I had made some dumb packing mistakes. I brought a journal. But did I really need to bring the whole hardcover journal? A few pieces of notebook paper would have sufficed. I brought squeezy tubes of smushed fruit. Too heavy. Rookie mistake. I could only learn and do better next time.

Huginnin Cove remained shrouded in fog for my two-night visit, cutting me off from everything and everyone. The gray water of Lake Superior disappeared into the mist. The ghostly silhouettes of peaked pines bordered the cove's edges. The island's magic wrapped me in sheer peace, like a rescuer draping a blanket over an accident victim's shoulders. I relished the opportunity to simply exist and be present.

There was no world beyond the cove. I made it, I thought. I'm here. I fucking did it.

The first night I awoke to the ground shaking as a moose thundered through my site, mere feet from me. Earlier, I made sure not to set up my tent on the moose trail that went through the site. Moose have poor eyesight, and I didn't want to get stepped on by a forest giant roaming in the night. In the morning, I sat on a rock, braiding my hair at the water's edge, and spied two moose across the cove. Nature kept on giving.

My five nights on the island were divided between Huginnin Cove and Washington Creek, near Windigo. The island had gifted me so many moose encounters that I stopped counting at about the fifteenth. The trip had been all mine.

* * *

Mere weeks after Isle Royale, I had a secret encounter with Mitch. Unbelievable, I know. I didn't want to go. But yet, I did want to go. I hovered over the edge of a cliff, ready to jump but still reaching back. Reaching for something that wasn't real. No matter how much I had wanted it to be. I knew it was craziness.

Like our meet-up two months earlier, I went through the motions of intimacy that I had mistaken for love, convinced I was done. This is it. For real this time. I'm ready, I thought. The fog was clearing. Not clear enough to see the horizon, but the road home was visible. The sex-only arrangement we'd been doing for the last ten months had been as detrimental to me as being in a full relationship. Poison was poison. A drop was as deadly as a whole bottle. Addiction in toxic relationships was real. My brain had worked against me. Mitch had crushed my spirit, and I had abandoned myself. But did I really? A new truth began to emerge. Maybe I had never developed a full sense of self to begin with. How could I abandon something I never had?

I backed out of Mitch's driveway and would never return.

I hit the trail the next day with new dedication, wrapping up two more counties over Labor Day weekend. That brought me to three hundred completed trail miles. During the months of walking those three hundred miles I had received five hundred emails from Mitch and spent four days with him. Over eight hundred miles lay ahead. His emails would keep coming, but I would never again choose to see Mitch.

* * *

He, however, would choose to see me. Eight days later, I sat on my porch planning my next trip out on the trail when Mitch pulled into the driveway. He knew my house was off-limits. I remained quiet as he walked over and sat in the white rocker that had been his to occupy when we were actively together. I wondered if his visit meant he had sensed my emotional distance during our last couple of times together.

"Can you come over again in a few days?" he asked.

"I'll be out on the trail," I said, nodding to the notebook on my lap, "I'm planning my next trip out." He paused for a moment. A pause I recognized as one that preceded drama.

"So." he said. More dramatic pause. "You think that doing segments on the Ice Age Trail is more important than being with me?" Irritation rose in his voice.

"Yes. I do." I said. A firm, clear yes. Not a half-hearted 'yeah' or a wishy-washy 'uh huh'. End it now, I thought. It's time. "And I won't be seeing you anymore," I added without explanation.

I had explained enough. Again and again, break-up attempt after break-up attempt, I had expressed my feelings. I had told him that his behavior was hurtful. And he always twisted the problem back to me. His behavior was my fault.

"Fuck you," he said, glaring at me. His breathing quickened which I had learned was a sign of brewing rage.

He swore at me again with more emphasis. His vile words flipped a switch. I shut down and my protective walls flew up. My eyes glazed over and I went dead inside. It's what I'd learned to do when someone spewed their verbal vomit on me. He cursed me again, looking irritated by my lack of response. Still, I numbly sat there. He stood over me.

"FUCK YOU, YOLANDA."

I did nothing. I felt nothing. It never occurred to me to get up and walk away. He repeated it again, standing over me. Behind my glazed eyes and frozen exterior, my heart raced.

He stepped off my porch and onto the front lawn, tantruming like a giant toddler. "FUCK YOU!!!" His eyes turned wild. The crazed eyes of rage. He screamed it again and again until he got into his car and sped off. I let out a deep sigh, not realizing I had been holding my breath.

I was done with his madness.

Part Two

I have a right to:

not have lies told about me.
not be stalked on the internet.
not have him show up at my house.
come home and not see gifts left at my door.
not have to wonder what I'll find in my email.
not receive mail accusing me of having an affair.
not have stories told about me after interactions with men.
not be told that things didn't happen the way I experienced them.
not be on the receiving end of another's rage.
not have my belongings stolen or destroyed.
not be emotionally torn down.
live my life in peace.
seek joy.

9

Mitch will not easily go away. I know him too well.

Dark clouds hung low in Taylor County, creating a landscape of soft, muted hues as I hiked through the woods and the edges of farm fields. The raindrops battering my poncho were my only company. The dreary day matched my mood. I was still shaken after the altercation with Mitch. The emotional stress of those moments with him took days of recovery. My mind and body stayed in high adrenaline mode, robbing me of peace.

I walked the trail with a new purpose. The wishy-washy voice that so many times had said, "I don't really want to be in this relationship anymore," transitioned to, "I won't be in this relationship anymore." Overnight, the trail had gone from being an enjoyable pastime, to a necessity for curing my confusing addiction. The hours and days spent on the trail so far had given me the courage to let go for good. Now I needed it to keep me from going back. The trail was also an escape. I hoped that if I wasn't around, Mitch would eventually go away. The old if-I-ignore-the-problem-it-will-disappear trick. But I knew better. He was not going to give up.

I assumed the best way to break my addiction was to remove myself from the addictive source. That became the plan. I needed to account for my time. Either be at work for twelve-hour shifts, on the trail, or traveling, with days committed to trail/travel prep/kids. No free days allowed. No room for "just one more time."

The barrage of emails, gifts, and cards would arrive, as they always did after an "incident". Mitch began emailing almost immediately after leaving my front porch. Within a couple of days, he placed flowers over my backyard fence. I tossed them into the trash and didn't respond. Many of his emails were sent minutes apart, with the tone drastically changing like someone flipping TV channels, going from game shows to horror movies to sitcoms. One email's subject line read: *The Danger in Camping Alone*.

You need to carry pepper spray or bear spray or at least an air horn in your tent. If a predator targets you while you are camping, after you are sexually assaulted in the privacy of your tent (most likely 1:30 or 2:00am) (waiting until other campers are fast asleep, but not so late cuz he will need the aid of darkness to cover his tracks) he will cut your throat. He cannot risk being identified by you. The penalties are too severe for sexual assault, and there is no death penalty in Wisconsin for a murderer. With the modern science of DNA, he cannot risk his DNA being found on or in your person. Your body will disappear. He will also remove your tent and its contents, burning these (at his convenience—there's no real hurry in attending to that detail) so as to leave no trace of his DNA there as well. You used to write dark stories. You don't want to be in one. Be smart and be prepared with one or more lines of defense. Your life depends on it.

When you live with insanity, you don't see it anymore. Throughout our relationship he had delved into ugly territory that I had normalized because of our twisted dance. What I didn't understand was that normalizing his behavior turned off my internal warning system for detecting potential danger. Someone in a healthy place would have read that message and said, "That's some crazy-ass shit… and a threat." I read that and thought, that's just Mitch.

I needed to stop engaging with Mitch in his emails. Stop trying to be heard. Stop looking to understand us. No contact. Just like my friend had once advised as being necessary to end a relationship with someone like Mitch. Communication must be cut off. Exactly a year ago, I sat in the police station and promised the officer I would not contact Mitch. I blew it. And I continued to blow it. Who would believe I wanted out of the relationship if I kept going back? I deserved to hear every question asking why. So no one knew. People keep secrets all the time to avoid shame.

Because of my previous failed attempts at leaving, I felt law enforcement or the court would not take me seriously and grant a restraining order. I needed written proof of my clear intentions to end it. My new plan was to stay silent regarding Mitch's emails, except for a few responses stating that I didn't want him contacting me anymore. It wasn't true no-contact, but I needed to do it that way so there would be no question about my stance. With multiple failures already under my belt, I needed to get my act together before receiving outside help.

* * *

I made an appointment to see a counselor, hoping it would help reinforce my commitment to stay away from Mitch. Someone to hold me accountable. Sort of like an alcoholic going to AA. Years ago, during my separation from my late husband, I sought counseling and found it helpful in gaining self-awareness and personal growth. But my new counselor wasn't grasping the situation with Mitch.

"Mitch will soon move on and be someone else's problem," she said with assurance.

I knew better. Mitch was not a problem that would easily go away. I don't have the right to say Mitch had a personality disorder, but I had the right to suspect he might. I had read that many therapists often didn't have the training to deal with domestic situations involving personality disorders. Wausau was considered rural in regards to healthcare, which could make it difficult to find therapists trained to meet certain needs. My problem with Mitch was more than a guy being a jerk during a breakup and me needing to heal a broken heart.

I needed someone to acknowledge that what I was going through was real. The situation had grown into something bigger than I could handle alone. Please. Listen to me. I don't know what to do, I wanted to say. But never having learned that it was okay to have my own voice, I didn't have the know-how to express my needs. Somehow, I ended up believing it wasn't okay for me to have needs. After three sessions, I didn't return. The trail would have to be my accountability partner. Taking a deeper look at myself would have to come later, after resolving the crushing issue of removing Mitch from my life.

* * *

November's gun deer hunting season was two months away. I didn't want to be in the Northwoods during that time. Not only for safety reasons, but to let the hunters have their nine days in the woods. I set a goal of finishing the northern sections before opening day. That made two goals to strive for: stay away from Mitch and complete northern Wisconsin by gun deer hunting.

SQUATTER

I headed to the Chippewa Moraine area, a couple of counties to the west. Its gentle hills and kettle lakes were the artwork of glacial ice that had towered between one and two miles thick. In one six-mile stretch of the trail, twenty-one lakes and ponds dotted the wooded landscape. Road options for bike shuttling through the Chippewa Moraine were few. That county chose not to offer shuttle rides during Covid, leaving me no choice but to bike.

For the longer bike routes, I leapfrogged: bike, hike, pick up bike, return, bike on farther, repeat. That meant more work of handling the bike, but it kept me closer to Fiona in case I had problems with the twenty-five-year-old Schwinn. I didn't know anything about making minor bicycle repairs.

I entered the trail, marveling at the lakes, glittering through the changing colors of the Chippewa Moraine forest. Kettle lakes sparkled around every bend. Maybe a giant, like in children's picture books, had once walked through the forest, scattering handfuls of diamonds that melted into delicate, shimmering lakes.

After the nearly two-hour drive from Wausau, biking eleven miles and hiking nine, I was done for the day. I checked Google for restaurants in the area. Mask mandates were in effect. I was willing to eat somewhere during non-peak hours and support restaurants during Covid. At four o'clock in the afternoon, I ate dinner in the empty Casa Mexicana restaurant in Bloomer.

"Thanks for coming in," my eager server said. Being a hospital nurse during Covid caused stress from the uncertainty we faced, but I still had a good income coming in. I left a generous tip.

Morris-Erickson County Park on Long Lake would be my home for the night. Eighteen dollars. Free sounded better. I rolled past the life-size silhouette of Bigfoot guarding the entrance, wrote out a check, and slipped it into the slot of a metal tube. Two RVs sat parked side by side in the far corner of the campground. I picked a spot and put up my tent without the rainfly. Sunset looked like it was promising to be a show. I waded into the cool water of Long Lake to watch. Smoke from Western wildfires transformed the sun into an orb suspended in milky haze. A loon's haunting call carried across the lake.

I crawled into my tent and checked my spam email. Mitch pressed me for a response to the flowers. *Did you receive the flowers? Yes or no?* I did not respond.

Up before dawn, I studied the day's plans over oatmeal and coffee: bike ten hilly miles and hike twelve. On the drive to the trailhead, a sliver of sun peeked over a hill. An encore of last night's performance. The otherworldly red globe hung in the pearly white sky.

The day was a repeat of hiking past diamond lakes created by the roaming giant. In mid-afternoon, I drove to pick up my bike on 245th Avenue. Someone had placed a sticky note on my bike seat. *Hope you enjoyed your hike.* A perfectly friendly message. But who was leaving Post-it notes in the middle of nowhere?

Unease gripped me. I glanced around to see if someone was watching me, as I fumbled with my bike lock. Maybe someone lurked behind the trees waiting for me to read it and then…bam…they'd jump out of the woods. A taunting message from an ax murderer.

I ran with my bike toward Fiona, while frantically turning my head in every direction. Was someone sneaking up behind me? From across the road? My breathing quickened and my heart raced as I scanned the woods. I lifted my

SQUATTER

bike into Fiona's bed and climbed in. I stood to assess my surroundings before laying down the bike in just the right way it needed to be to close the tailgate.

Maybe Mitch's message about getting my throat cut was true. Maybe I would die out here by myself.

Bullshit.

The voice of reason pushed away the unpleasant scenario in favor of a benign explanation. Except, I couldn't come up with a benign explanation at that moment. I refused to let his scare tactics destroy me. I hopped down out of the truck bed, jumped into the front seat, and hit the gas pedal, leaving a cloud of dust to dissipate in the woods.

At home later that night, I posted pictures in the Facebook group. The county's trail coordinator had been at various trailheads that day and left the message on my bike. There was no ax murderer.

I couldn't let Mitch's words get into my head and scare me away from my adventure.

10

I'll admit that sometimes the thought crosses my mind about stumbling upon danger in the woods.

My inability to hike big miles bothered me. I'd always been fairly fit, but never an athlete. In junior high, we had to run the dreaded nine-minute mile in gym class. I'd worry about it for days until the horrible moment arrived. My friends weren't runners, but seemed to do fine. I had been an active kid. Played outside. Rode my bike. Walked. But, when it came to upping the intensity, I couldn't hack it. I'd be red-faced, breathless, and near tears.

After all the hiking and biking miles I'd put in, I was disappointed in being unable to regularly do high-mileage days. I chided myself. That damn bone pain. I didn't want to drive a couple of hours from home to do a daily eight miles. Mileage days in the teens were doable. I didn't love it, but I could do multiple days in a row of that mileage. How do some hikers walk twenty-plus miles day after day? Yeah, I did those two twenty-something mile days early on and they practically killed me. My fitness level should have risen enough to regularly do twenty-something mile days by now. But it hadn't. I tried not to dwell on my perceived limitations. But, when I'd squat down to bring relief to my legs, or do that weird old-person walk while mumbling, "Oh my gosh," I felt like that out of breath, red-faced girl who couldn't run with the rest.

* * *

My hiking poles came. I had visited an outdoorsy store's website and purchased a two-hundred-dollar pair for a hundred bucks. I couldn't wait to try them out. After a late start for the two-and-a-half-hour drive west, I laid my new poles across my bike's rear carrying rack and pedaled off for the one-hour shuttle ride. The McKenzie Creek segment was over nine miles. Sunset would be at seven sharp. Rocks and roots lay hidden in leaves and grass all along the northern part of the trail. I carried a headlamp in my pack, but navigating the rugged trail would still be risky in the dark. I had four hours of daylight to get it done.

I dawdled to photograph McKenzie Creek, then got cruising through a forest decorated with near-peak fall color. My balance and agility made up for my other physical limitations. Even before using my poles, I had easily navigated rough terrain, dancing across streams on rocks and logs without missing a beat. The poles made it even easier. I still had pain after hitting the eight-mile wall, but the sun hugging the horizon motivated me to keep up the pace.

The woods darkened. I still had two miles to go. Dogs barked in the distance. Their barking wasn't stationary as if coming from a farmyard. They were on the move through the woods. I picked up the pace, my stomach twisting at the thought of being overtaken by hunting dogs, stray dogs, or whatever kind of dogs. My breathing changed from the working-my-body-hard kind of breaths to anxiety breaths. I recalled the story of the first Ice Age Trail thru-hiker, Jim Staudacher. During his 1979 hike, he was attacked by the leader of a feral dog pack. He had grabbed a piece of wood from his campfire and beat the dog to death. The rest of the pack retreated. I didn't have the strength to fend off an attacking dog but bear spray hung on my belt. Would that be enough to deter multiple dogs, I wondered. My hiking poles helped me to fly through the woods. The barking grew louder. And closer. Breathless, I pushed through the last mile as darkness settled.

My plan was to camp at a dispersed camping area (DCA) that wasn't far from the road. I drove to where Guthook said there should be parking, but didn't see any. Even if I parked on the side of the road, I wasn't comfortable walking into unfamiliar woods at night to search for the DCA.

The town of Luck was down the road where Cafe Wren allowed hikers to camp on their property. Google said they were already closed. I dialed, hoping someone was still there. No answer.

Google also showed a city campground in Luck. I followed the street that led to a large, grassy area with a bathroom building. It was approaching eight o'clock and the campground office was closed. I decided to stay anyway. I unloaded my gear by moonlight when voices erupted from a canvas tent set up next to the bathrooms.

"You're such a fucking loser!" a woman's voice shouted. "You're just a nuthin!"

A male voice muffled a response that I couldn't make out.

"No! I won't be quiet! I don't care if someone's here!" the woman yelled, slurring her words. "Why did I get stuck with such a loser?!"

Ouch. So painful. How embarrassing for the man. He left the tent and slunk down the road with his head hung low. His hunched shoulders carried the weight of defeat. A defeat I knew well. Does he ask himself, "What's wrong with me?" I wondered if he heard shameful messages as a kid. Funny how that cycle works. Just because our brain normalizes something, doesn't mean it's good.

I lowered the tailgate and boiled water in my Jetboil for dinner. Clouds smothered the moonlight and sprinkles fell as my dried meal rehydrated. I ate in the truck. Then it was time to use the women's room, its entrance steps away from the couple's tent.

The man had returned from his walk. They sat under the tent's awning, looking like a happy couple enjoying the evening with a bottle of wine. They smiled and nodded to me. I did the same. Signals acknowledging that we were playing the game of feigning amnesia about the unpleasant encounter. I suppose we all erect a facade of normalcy in order to hide the pain of what happens behind closed doors. The couple remained silent for the rest of the night.

I packed up the tent at morning twilight. Using the bathroom wasn't an option that morning. The woman and her so-called loser partner had clearly moved past the previous evening's turmoil. Their tent rigorously rocked and swayed to the rhythmic moans of passion as I drove away.

* * *

September ended, taking along the summer's warmth. Mitch's emails continued to pour in. I read them because I was used to that connection. He professed his love, explained his behavior, wrote about staining his fence, sent information about the Isle Royale Winter Study, and pointed out things in nature that were shaped like a Y for Yolanda. He was attempting to lure me into the honeymoon, reconciliation stage of the cycle. The abuse cycle. There. I admitted it. The merry-go-round we had ridden for the last few years was the abuse cycle.

I returned to a blaze of color in western Wisconsin on an afternoon in early October. Wearing my puffy jacket, I began the bike shuttle. The soft gravel roads took me past faded signs marking the sites of old one-room schoolhouses. Shady Dell School 1915-1941. Mound School 1917-1951. I pedaled by, imagining life during a time when these schoolhouses dotted the countryside.

At five o'clock, I locked up my bike at the trailhead and entered the five-and-a-half mile Indian Creek segment. No roaming dogs in the woods would disrupt my hike that evening. Freshly fallen leaves, with their musky sharp aroma, carpeted the ground, hiding the trail. Autumn moments like that, when both trees and forest floor become an artist's palette of warm colors, are fleeting. I'd spend the next three days in that exquisite northern Wisconsin autumnal beauty.

A sliver of orange spanning the horizon was all that remained of the day when I picked up my bike. Another night of pitching the tent in the dark. I had permission to camp on the same lake property where Laura and I had stayed back in August. I turned onto the narrow, private drive that led through the woods. I anticipated crossing the little Tonka truck bridge. I didn't need to go all the way to the lake. Darkness had already set in and I'd be up before the sun.

Up ahead the path widened to accommodate a flatbed trailer and a log pile. A perfect spot to stop for the night. I'd gotten used to being alone in the dark woods. But, I still practiced what I started on that first solo camping trip to Rock Island: keeping my focus on where the light shone and not looking out into the dark. I lowered the tailgate to make dinner. My headlamp illuminated my Jetboil and I added

SQUATTER

boiling water to the dried meal. Afterwards, I snuggled in my sleeping bag and waited for sleep to come.

My eyes flew open at an unfamiliar sound next to my tent. What the fuck? It's incredible how fast one can go from a sound sleep to a state of high alert. I held my breath and lay paralyzed, my eyes wide open to the darkness. The sound definitely came from an animal. Like a crying or stressed animal, but nothing I could identify. It leapt away, and I knew it had to be a deer. But why did it make that bleating noise? I didn't hear anything else indicating another animal was nearby. Maybe I made a noise in my sleep and startled it. I stayed on high alert until I couldn't fight sleep any longer.

I peeked out of my sleeping bag in the morning darkness and breathed icy air. I sealed the bag around my neck to hold in the warmth while my face adjusted to the frosty sting. The weather report said the night's low would be twenty-nine degrees. I could tell without looking that it was correct. I reluctantly sat up, braced myself for the cold, and dressed in layers for the day. The sky turned pink as I drove to the trailhead, passing fields draped in fog. I lowered the tailgate to make a breakfast of oatmeal, cranberries, powdered goat milk, and coffee. Juan Valdez instant coffee was what Mitch used for camping and what I continued to buy for myself. I'd come to associate its flavor with the outdoors.

I bundled up for a long bike shuttle on soft dirt roads and pedaled to the Sand Creek trailhead. Portions of the segment followed old logging roads with areas of massive mud pits. An hour into my hike, I approached a car stuck in one of those pits, one back tire submerged in mud. A pickup truck sat ahead of the car, having made it through the mud pit. A man sat in the truck with the window down.

"This looks pretty sucky," I said. "Do you have help coming?"

"Yeah...waitin' on a buddy to come with chains," the man answered.

"Hope your day gets better," I replied and continued walking.

Finishing Sand Creek also meant completing another county. Some of the Ice Age Trail counties and chapters awarded patches for completing their area; most of those chapters were in the southern portion of the state. This county would be my first patch. A prize! As a kid in the seventies, I longed for "junk cereal", as my mom called it-- not only for the yummy sugar content, but also for the prize pictured on the box. But we always bought Shredded Wheat. No prizes in Shredded Wheat. Bazooka Bubble gum with the comic strip wrappers? Nope. Trident. Plain ol' wrappers with Trident. I couldn't wait for my prize to come in the mail...while Shredded Wheat sat in my cupboard and Trident rested at the bottom of my purse. All kinds of things follow us from childhood.

I parked at the Timberland Hills trailhead for lunch. I brought something new for trail meals, thinking I'd raise my trail food up a notch. Garlic risotto. The instructions said to add the bagged contents to boiling water. I figured why not reverse it and add boiling water to the bag like the packaged trail meals. While my fancy risotto rehydrated, I ate a granola bar. And then checked the risotto. Still watery. After eating a squeezy tube of carrot, zucchini, and pear mush, I checked it again. Still watery. I sat on the tailgate, swinging my legs and sipping coffee, waiting to enjoy my gourmet lunch.

SQUATTER

A Subaru pulled up to the trailhead. Irritation swept over me, like how dare these people enter my space. I had gotten used to having most everything regarding the trail to myself. The feeling surprised me a bit. The trail wasn't mine. But as much solitude that I'd experienced in the last few hundred miles, it sure felt like it. A gray-haired couple exited the car. They were from Madison and had come to hike and enjoy the fall colors. They asked about my plans.

"You camped out here in the cold last night?" the gentleman asked.

"Oh my goodness, you are brave. I need a hot shower and a hamburger after hiking," the lady said as she smiled. I glanced at my saggy bag of rice. We wished each other an enjoyable rest of the day. They entered the trail and I hopped on my bike.

The Timberland Hills segment followed along cross-country ski trails through county forests. The lack of forest roads made for a long bike shuttle around the county forest perimeter. To conquer the long ride, I leapfrogged the afternoon (the bike, hike, repeat scenario). I left the bagged risotto with Fiona to hopefully become edible. After returning from the first hike, I checked the rice. Finally done. I took a bite. It was freaking cold. I'm eating cold mush. I thought about the hamburger the Madison lady would be eating after her hike, and continued to think about it for the rest of the afternoon.

Cell service along the county highway allowed me to search for camping options. Camping options near hamburgers. The town of Shell Lake was fifteen minutes away, with a city campground on the lake. Hamburgers were nearby.

I pulled into the campground. Signs on the bathroom and park office doors read, *Closed for Covid*. The office door sign said camping was permitted but there were no open bathroom facilities. Instructions were to register at City Hall before four-thirty. It was almost five. Well...I wasn't parking a camper that sucked electricity or needed to be dumped. No bathroom access. So, I thought free sounded good. I would return to set up my tent after my hamburger.

I pulled up to a cozy diner a few blocks away. After putting on my mask, I opened the door. The place was packed. The room fell silent as every eye turned toward me: The person with the mask. I stood in the doorway wearing my blaze-orange hat, gray hiking pants, and gray hoodie that read Where the Heck is Truth or Consequences? (the name of a real town in New Mexico where daughter-in-law number two was from). Part of me wanted to leave. This is too crowded, I thought. Covid numbers were rising fast. But a bigger part of me wanted that hamburger. I spied an empty stool at the end of the counter.

I gingerly stepped between the tables of the hushed room while eyes followed me. After I took the stool next to an elderly gentleman, chatter and the clinking of utensils resumed. Almost as if on cue, like someone had announced the show was over. I smiled and nodded at the gentleman before turning my back to create space between us. I savored a hamburger and hot chocolate heaped with whipped cream before heading back to the city park, expecting a cool night in the thirties.

* * *

The sky held its first hint of light while I made breakfast at the trailhead, overlooking a field facing the east. Heavy cloud cover hid the sunrise. The morning would be a nine-mile

SQUATTER

bike shuttle around the borders of the county forest in order to hike the last five miles of Timberland Hills. I bundled up in layers and pedaled off. The crisp, morning air stung my face as I coasted down a hill. Fog rose over a lake to my right. I stopped to watch a pair of trumpeter swans; two apparitions floating in the mist. Partners at peace.

I locked up my bike and entered Timberland Hills on the grassy ski trails. Four mounds of fresh bear scat sat in a row along the trail. I wasn't the only one on the move early that morning. The scat didn't make me nervous. Bears were in the woods whether or not I saw their scat. After an hour or so of following along a grassy road, I approached some sort of camp. Not a campground camp, but a something-sketchy-might-be-going-on-in-the-woods kind of camp. A couple of rusty cars, a large canvas tent, and random junk sat in a dip amongst the trees. Two protective dogs charged me. I pointed my hiking poles in their direction, anticipating them jumping on me. A man from the camp called them back before they reached me.

"What's up?" he gruffly asked. He wore a dirty Carhartt jacket and did not look happy to see me.

"Where's the trail?" I asked, scanning the trees for a yellow blaze.

"What trail?" His tone was curt and intense.

His lack of knowledge about the trail that was right under his nose concerned me. Even though I didn't dwell on the possible negative aspects of solo adventuring, the unfortunate scenario of stumbling upon shady shenanigans going on deep in the forest was something that crossed my mind at times.

"The Ice Age Trail...I'm following the Ice Age Trail... with yellow marks on the trees," I answered while smiling big, trying to give off a pleasant, non-threatening vibe, letting him know I wasn't there to bother him or snoop in his business. The grim scene from the movie Fargo--of the body being pushed through the woodchipper-- flashed through my mind.

"I dunno no Ice Age Trail," he said, squinting his eyes as if he were trying to discern whether or not I was telling the truth.

I smiled even bigger and pulled out my phone to check Guthook, not only to see if I missed a turn but to prove to him that I was really hiking a trail and not snooping around. "See..." I tilted my phone toward him. Then I noticed that the little arrow indicating my location didn't line up with the trail. Sure enough, quite a ways back, I missed a sharp turn where the trail left the grassy road for a footpath.

"I'm really sorry for inconveniencing you," I said. He lightened up a bit.

"Yeah, I'm sorry for coming off kinda rough. Ya never know who's wanderin' around out here," he said. "Have a good day."

He had been as leery of me as I was of him. I made my way back to the trail, glancing over my shoulder multiple times.

11

I like to think that people from other times and places have had similar experiences to mine. We're all connected.

I returned to western Wisconsin a few days later and planned to squeeze in a road walk before setting up camp. I pedaled nearly six miles, left the bike, and returned on foot as the disappearing sun turned blaze-orange. I arrived at dusk in the town of Haugen.

All was still and quiet with Haugen's 287 residents tucked away in their homes. The town was an early-to-bed, early-to-rise kind of place. Work needed to be done when the sun rose. Inviting warmth illuminated the windows of the town's homes. As I passed each home, I witnessed a moment in that household's life: someone clearing the table after dinner, someone washing dishes, another sitting in their living room staring at the television's blue glow.

Ahead stood a brick building with a white ice chest and soda machines guarding the front. *Hill's Village Grocery* was written in faded paint on the building's side. I had made a sandwich for dinner that waited for me in Fiona. But milk and chips also sounded good. It was almost seven o'clock. I hoped they were still open.

Pumpkins and gourds adorned the store's entrance. *Fire Warden–Burning Permits Issued*, a sign declared. Another simply said, *Worms and Crawlers*. A wooden shelf, loaded with vegetables and trinkets for sale, sat next to the soda machine. Two Packer t-shirts hung from a white chain that spanned across the front of the shelf. A handwritten cardboard sign reading, *Vegetables Fresh From Dave's Organic Garden*, also dangled from the chain, clipped with a clothespin. I guessed that everyone in town knew Dave.

I pushed open the door, triggering a little bell announcing my arrival. No one was at the front counter. I walked back to the coolers for milk. An older couple, maybe Mr. and Mrs. Hill, ate dinner in the back of the store. They watched a small tv that sat on a folding card table. Their friendly aura led me to believe that they played a grandparenting role to children both related to them and those in need of a grandparent's wisdom and love.

"Can I help you find anything?" the presumed Mrs. Hill asked.

"Just a single serving size of milk," I answered. With milk in hand, I followed her to the counter and grabbed a bag of chips.

"Are you hiking the trail?" she asked as she rang up my purchases. When I told her yes, she handed me a notebook. "Please sign our register. We like to see how many hikers come into the store."

I walked out of Haugen, eating the chips and milk. The thin, red line on the horizon offered the last moments of light for the day. In the near darkness that robbed the world of color, everything turned to shadows, and the outlines of headstones came into view. A looming iron gate arched over a cemetery's entrance. I imagined entering a gothic novel scene as the gate stood eerily outlined against the blackening sky. The words *Cesky Narodni Hrbitov* were embedded in the arches' decorative swirls. A wave of Czech immigrants settled in Wisconsin during the mid-nineteenth century. A wooden sign faced the road. I shined my flashlight in its direction. *Bohemian National Cemetery Est. 1897.* There were more words, but my phone's flashlight couldn't illuminate the smaller print from where I stood. I walked through the grass and read a message from beyond the grave: *What you are we once were. What we are you will be.*

The names etched in the headstones were once people like us. They lived life. They experienced our same feelings. They birthed babies and raised children. They felt exasperation when four-year-olds asked their hundredth question. They gossiped about neighbors but lent a helping hand during trying times. There were those who worked hard and those who were lazy. They found true love as well as partaking in secret affairs with other people's true loves. They had close, caring families as well as distant, broken ones. They weren't just names etched in a tombstone. They were us. Just us from a different time.

I walked on in the soupy darkness that can only be found in the country. Deer surrounded me. Their hooves clattered on the road, but the night blinded me to their form. Other mysterious nocturnal creatures rustled in the fields and woods as I passed. I loved moving unseen and unknown through the night.

A car approached from a bend up ahead. A woman walking a remote road at night would be an unusual sight. Most likely they'd drive by. Or the driver might stop to see if I needed help and I'd have to go through the whole awkward spiel of, "I'm hiking the Ice Age Trail…yeah, I know this is a road not a trail…but road walks are part of the trail." The worst case scenario would be I'd disappear, after being in the wrong place at the wrong time. I chose to step into the woods until they passed.

I reached Fiona at eight o'clock. As her headlights illuminated the forest, a case of the willies came over me. Nothing was there to fear. It was an irrational feeling. After all, I'd just walked miles in the dark completely unafraid. But something about shining light into the dark woods bothered me. Maybe it's a phobia. Maybe I thought the light would reveal unseen scary things. While eating my sandwich, I drove to Shell Lake to spend the night in the little city campground.

* * *

I got to the trailhead before sunrise and ate breakfast in the morning chill. No bike shuttling today. The chapter coordinator for the area dropped me off for a sixteen-mile day. I wasn't far into the Bear Lake segment when a fox darted across the trail. I fumbled for my phone to capture a photo, but with his red coat, he disappeared into the October foliage.

I passed four hundred miles. One-third of the trail was completed. I hadn't seen Mitch in over thirty days. Nor had I responded to his continuing emails. If I didn't stay the course, the cycle would continue.

With no long morning bike ride, my hiking day ended mid-afternoon. After a fish fry at Shell Lake's Lakeview Bar and Grill, in their socially distanced dining room, I once again headed to the city campground. I chose a spot along the lakeshore instead of the shelter of the trees. After setting up my tent, thunder rumbled in the distance. I checked the radar on my phone. A red blob headed my way. I wasn't confident that the stakes would keep my tent grounded in high wind. The weight of my sleeping bag and pad wouldn't be enough to keep a wind gust from blowing my tent into the lake. I tied the tent strings to the picnic table and hopped back into Fiona as the dark sky let loose a deluge. The stakes held tight and the tent's survival didn't come down to the strings attached to a table.

The storm passed, leaving behind light sprinkles. I fell asleep looking forward to the easy day I'd have on the Tuscobia rail/trail segment. Rail/trails are old railroad grades that had been cut through the landscape at the most level area possible. The Ice Age Trail followed along multiple recreational rail/trails around the state. Since they're recreational trails, I could bike them and not fuss with searching for an alternative route. A few weeks ago, I flew down the crushed limestone of the Gandy Dancer rail/trail segment on my bike. I anticipated the same for Tuscobia.

Venus twinkled in the black morning sky, reflecting on Shell Lake. I rolled up my wet tent and tossed it into the truck's backseat. Doing the trail with Fiona made me happy. She offered shelter, heat, space for my stuff and her tailgate breakfasts couldn't be beat.

The Tuscobia segment shared eleven miles of the seventy-four mile Tuscobia State rail/trail. On the map, I eyed the two-and-a-half-mile road walk that followed. An easy add-on. I hopped on my bike before sunrise and bounced along the rough, grassy trail. It wasn't the crushed limestone I had expected. Maybe this is an odd spot, I thought. It'll get better.

The washboard trail shook me like the people in old-time movie clips wearing those weird vibrating belts to lose weight. What kind of bike trail was this? My anticipated easy bike shuttle became an exercise in misery. I could walk as fast as I was able to bike the treacherous trail. After a two-hour beating on the path from hell, I finished the eleven miles. Two hours to bike just over eleven miles. Embarrassing stats. Screw the connecting route, I thought. I'll pick up here next time. I locked my bike to a tree and in a steaming huff, began my return walk.

As the morning dragged on, visions of a second breakfast filled my mind. Rail/trails pass through towns and villages just as trains did years ago. The village of Brill was a couple of miles ahead. They must have a diner. Every cute little town has a diner, I reasoned.

I left the trail and walked into Brill on 23 ¼ Street, which was basically the only street in town. The lone street looked more like a deserted movie set. A Pabst Blue Ribbon sign creaked in the breeze as it swayed from a building with a tall false front. A granary across from the bar loomed over the street. Its whitewashed platform, which must have welcomed generations of farmers, now stood empty. There were no eggs and sausage here. With a heavy sigh, I returned to the trail.

I wasn't giving up on my second breakfast. I had passed a closed diner back in Haugen the night before. A quick zoom-in on Google said that it was Lona's Cafe. I dialed their number. They were open until two o'clock. Yes, they still had dine-in AND they served breakfast all day. The time was 11:30 and I had four-and-a-half miles to go. From the trailhead it was only a three-mile drive to Lona's Cafe. I'd pick my bike up after eating. Eggs and sausage were in my future after all.

I pulled into the cafe an hour before closing time. A hand-painted wooden sign adorned with white polka-dotted red mushrooms greeted me: *Welcome to Lona's Corner Cafe.* In a patch of grass, sat wooden, pumpkin cutouts leaning against a metal pail filled with dried mums that were past their prime. Through the window, I saw two other diners.

Perfect. I wouldn't need my mask. I walked in and took a seat at the counter while exchanging a smiling nod with the two men at a nearby table.

I learned from eavesdropping that they were father and son. The topic of conversation was what most people talked about at the time. Covid.

"I don't know how we're going to make it if we comply with the 25% capacity rule," Lona said to the father and son. Last spring's 25% capacity rule was lifted over the summer and would soon be reinstated.

The father turned to me. "Are ya from the area?"

"No, I'm section-hiking the Ice Age Trail," I answered. "I've done over 400 miles so far."

"Alone?" Lona asked as she poured my coffee.

Lona and the two men asked the common questions people wanted to know when they heard that I was hiking the trail. What exactly is section-hiking? How do you section-hike by yourself? How long is the trail?

"Aren't you afraid of bears?" Lona asked.

"Not really. They try to avoid people. I'm just cautious… especially about meeting up with a mama and cub. If I was in grizzly country, I might be leerier," I answered.

"You're braver than me," Lona said.

Lona brought me what I craved: eggs, toast, and sausage. I ate every bite and then headed home. The next day would be spent grocery shopping and resting up before my three twelve-hour nursing shifts. Only three emails from Mitch. A light day for him.

I stuck with the plan. I did not respond.

12

Do I bear responsibility for someone else's actions? If so, how much?

The two segments through the Chequamegon National Forest, Jerry Lake, and Mondeaux Esker, totaled nearly twenty-seven miles. Bike routes looked to be painstakingly long. I made ride arrangements with Buzz, the county's coordinator, for two shuttle rides.

On a dark, mid-October morning, I tossed my bike into Fiona's bed and headed to the Jerry Lake trailhead just over an hour from home. I always brought my bike along in case shuttle plans fell through. The sun peeked over the horizon when I met Buzz at the trailhead. Buzz was known to be quite the trail hero of the Chequamegon. He not only gave shuttle rides, but has come to the rescue of hikers with sprained ankles, hypothermia, heat exhaustion, and broken wrists after falls. He even rescued a group who, after being dropped off, hiked in the opposite direction from where their car was parked.

I put on my mask and hopped into Buzz's truck. His smile was hidden behind the mask, but twinkled in his friendly eyes. We chatted, and I told him about the bleating sound I heard next to my tent a couple of weeks ago.

"Yup, deer make bleating noises," Buzz confirmed. "I've heard them plenty of times while out hunting."

SQUATTER

I didn't have that kind of outdoor background, nor was I raised around people who hunted. I sometimes wished I knew more about farming and hunting. They seemed like topics that united people.

"Thank you–see you tomorrow!" I said as my breath billowed out in the crisp morning air. The old-growth forest welcomed me into its magical world of giant white pines, meandering creeks, and stunning eskers–long, narrow ridges left behind by retreating glaciers. No cell service in the Chequamegon and I welcomed that barrier from Mitch.

I hit the eight-mile mark, and the groaning fest began. I stumbled on a rock hidden in the leaves which tweaked my knee. That slowed me down even more. I came to a wooden bridge spanning a creek, a good photo opportunity. My sore knee wouldn't keep me from taking the photographs that I wanted, so I squatted to get the right angle. Getting up from that position was a challenge that involved cursing and a bit of contortionism.

I was down to the last mile of my fifteen-mile day. Why was the last freakin' mile so hard? I've been doing the trail for seven months, and I even had poles. Eighty-year-old people run marathons for goodness' sake. A fifteen-mile day with a daypack shouldn't be hard. But for me, it was. And it pissed me off.

After eight hours, I finally made it to Fiona, who sat patiently waiting for me. I pulled off my hiking boots, changed into my Crocs, and popped an Aleve. I had a dried dinner with me, but wanted something yummier. I found cell service that led me to Cindy's Bar and Grill. And they were open.

I sat at the bar, joining the four others already there, and ordered the special of the day: chicken wings. That sounded fantastic. I checked my spam email. Three messages from Mitch. I wanted to cave in and see him. Can't he just love me like a normal person? But I walked a new path now. My dinner basket arrived from the kitchen in a flash. A frail, gray-haired gentleman with a mask walked in to pick up a to-go order. The others at the bar turned to greet him.

"Hey Ed!" one said with a wave. "How's Doris doin' these days?"

"Oh, gettin' along alright. Her hip's really botherin' her," Ed responded as he paid for his order. For a few minutes they all chatted about the everyday stuff of life. The stuff that connects people because what was someone else's problem today could be yours tomorrow. And they gathered in country bars like Cindy's to connect and enjoy a beer while doing so.

I had no idea where to camp when I pulled out of Cindy's parking lot and headed back to the Chequamegon. I had one hour until sunset to figure it out. Dispersed camping was allowed in the National Forest as long as you're two-hundred feet from a water source and one-hundred fifty-feet from the road.

I followed the forest road looking for a suitable place. Guthook showed parking up ahead. That would have to do because the sun was gone and twilight didn't penetrate the thick forest. I parked and let Fiona's headlights illuminate the dark while I set up my tent. Being near the Mondeaux Dam Recreation Area, the underbrush near the parking area was fairly clear, making it easy to set up. Hopefully I was one-hundred fifty feet from the road. With Covid, no one was coming around to check. I brushed my teeth and crawled into my sleeping bags. Yes, plural. The nights were growing colder, so I used two sleeping bags. I stuffed my regular bag, rated to twenty-five degrees, into a larger military cold-weather bag that my son had been issued in the Marine Corps.

The time was only 6:45. The Aleve had kicked in and my knee felt better. I had a camp light in the truck if I wanted to read. But it was too cold to take my hands out of the bag to hold a book. Plus, I didn't like the idea of having my tent be a beacon announcing, I'm here! So, I lay still, waiting for sleep to come, while listening to my breathing and for anything else that might indicate that I wasn't alone.

The sound of frozen pellets hitting the tent brought me out of a deep sleep. The side of my face had gotten cold. I pulled the bag over my head and fell back asleep. I woke up again just after five. "Holy shit," I mumbled as I sat up in the shockingly cold air, allowing my upper body to adjust. Sort of like inching into a cold pool. I slipped on my Crocs, unzipped the tent and stepped out into the blackness. Snow crunched beneath my feet. I was drawn to look to the sky. The stars called again. I left the shelter of the trees to find an open view of the sky. Heaven was alive with the flickering of thousands of stars. They brimmed with an energy that I absorbed while standing in the Chequamegon National Forest's October snow. I was doing the trail and sleeping alone in the woods. I could figure things out myself—and even do it on the fly.

Self-confidence was something that I had lacked my entire life. Enough so, that it crippled me. My out-of-control teen spiral had flung me into space. Then I landed to grow a family. Outwardly, I seemed steady during those years. But I still had no voice. Once in my late twenties, I was randomly chosen to be in a small group to discuss energy in our town. I remember it being less than twenty people. Maybe it was the electric company or something who wanted to hear from the community. They offered free food during the meeting, so I said sure. And I never spoke up. Not a word. The point of the group was to hear the concerns of the community, not to come and eat free food.

I remember coming across an old report card from early elementary school. The exact wording escapes me, but the teacher said in essence that I looked to the other kids for figuring things out. So, my lack of trust in my own judgment was there at a young age. Was I born broken? I watched the pulsating stars. Not one of them looked broken.

I packed up the tent and drove through the black forest. Fiona's headlights reflected off the fresh snow blanketing the woods. Experiencing the season's first snow while out on the trail thrilled me. I pulled up to the trailhead on Shady Drive--forest on one side, field on the other. I parked and began breakfast in the frigid darkness. Buzz would arrive in an hour. I had a magical hour to watch October 16, 2020 come into being over a snow-covered field in northern Wisconsin.

With a cup of warm coffee, I paced the road. Fog hugged the snow in the low-lying field. The ghostly mirages of three deer meandered through the mist, unconcerned with my presence. Maybe they were in awe of the first snow as well. Subtle changes on the horizon grounded me in the moment. The western sky remained black while the east surrendered the night. Brilliant oranges and reds pushed away the blackness and claimed the sky. A spot on the horizon blazed with flaming orange, announcing the soon arriving sun. I watched the day begin in solitude and marveled at the beauty of it all.

Buzz pulled up for my shuttle ride that would take me to the other end of the Mondeaux Esker.

SQUATTER

"It's a busy day for shuttles," Buzz said. The day was Friday, and October was a prime hiking month. Plus, Covid got people interested in outdoor activities.

Buzz dropped me off at the trailhead, where a couple of women were getting ready for their hike.

"Hey! You're the one with the bike and the truck!" said one of the women. "I follow your posts." They were heading the opposite way. We wished each other a good hike and I headed into the woods. The morning sunbeams glittered off the snow-covered pines and hardwoods. As the sun warmed the morning, the trees shed the white powder. Clumps of snow plopped down along the trail. Sometimes a clump would fall at the right moment, leaving me with an icy bath trickling down my back. By the time I reached the esker to walk along its spine, the snow had melted away, and the forest was once again a carpet of brown.

After passing last night's campsite, I crossed the Mondeaux Dam and entered the eastern portion of the segment, which was known for being muddy. It lived up to its reputation. Mud and tall, wet grass were themes for the rest of the day. The area lacked the stately trees of the segment's western side, as it was new forest growth with thick underbrush. Heavy, wet snow squalls blew through as I pulled out my rain jacket and put it over my puffy coat. I crossed streams on rickety beams and wet rocks. I exited the trail on Shady Drive. The field across the road where I witnessed the magical morning was now just another drab, brown, late-autumn scene in Wisconsin.

* * *

I backed out of my driveway in the early morning darkness of October 23 for the two-hour drive west. I would be meeting my shuttle ride on a dead-end road in the Blue Hills.

Early winter had arrived in northwestern Wisconsin and I drove down a snow-covered Stout Road during morning twilight. I had finished getting my daypack ready and laced up my boots when the headlights of a white pickup truck appeared. I checked to make sure I had my keys before locking Fiona. I had become compulsive about the keys, fearing that I would lock them in the truck and be stuck miles from anywhere without cell service.

"Do I see the keys?" I'd say.

Yes.

"Do I REALLY see them?"

Yes, they're in my hand.

Okay…locking the truck now…and I see the keys in my hand…I'm really going to lock it now…eyes are on the keys…I'm pressing the button. I put the keys in the same inner pocket of my pack. Every. Time. I didn't want a panicked moment of tearing apart my pack while saying, "Where did I put the keys this time?"

I put on my mask and hopped into the truck with Fred, the chapter coordinator. After the usual greetings, I mentioned I hadn't decided where to camp that night.

"I'd say Murphy Flowage—easy to access and just up the road a ways," Fred said.

"Then that's what I'll do. Locals know best," I replied.

Fred would be dropping me off fourteen miles away, on 28 ¾ Street, where I had locked up my bike after the Tuscobia bike shuttle nightmare. I remembered the oddly specific signs while walking through Brill searching for breakfast.

"Why are the streets numbered so specifically?" I asked Fred.

"It's the distance from the county seat. It helps first responders locate emergencies faster," Fred said.

SQUATTER

"Ahh, that makes sense. Good idea," I said as we arrived at my stop. "Thanks for the info and the ride. See you tomorrow morning!"

Heavy, wet snow fell as I walked 28 ¾ Street. I pulled up the hood of my Marmot coat. I passed 29 ⅞ Avenue. The short road walk passed quickly, and I entered the Hemlock Creek segment. The seven-mile segment would take me through the county forest. My foggy, wet glasses made it difficult to see, so I spent much of the hike with my head tipped in various directions to see where I was going. The snow had no plans in letting up. I had waterproofed both pairs of boots. That was useful to a point, but by mid-morning, my boots got heavier as they soaked up the trail's wet snow.

Snow clung to the trees, creating a world sung about in Christmas songs. I crossed snow-covered boardwalks and felt a little guilty for ruining the virgin snow. I came to one of the familiar brown Ice Age Trail posts. Bears liked the wood's stain, so I was used to seeing damage to the signs as a result of their gnawing. But the top of that post was torn to shreds—peeled back like a banana. Holy crap! I thought. Some bear really went to town on that. Or at least I assumed it was a bear. Maybe Bigfoot liked the stain as well.

Snow continued to dump from the sky at noon. I came to a log picnic shelter after crossing Hemlock Creek and sat inside to eat lunch. My feet were damp, and I still had about seven miles left. I crossed the county highway and entered the Northern Blue Hills segment. The day never brightened but remained a bleak, dark one filled with substantial snowfall. I faced a beastly afternoon. The trail lay submerged under muddy logging roads that were impossible to maneuver around on dry land. I gave up trying to keep my feet dry.

I came to a snow-covered beaver dam with open water behind it and pondered the beautiful scene. So much serenity. Before the trail, I had never heard of the Blue Hills. Now, I was deep within them, getting ready to step into the fresh snow blanketing a beaver dam. There was no way around it. The dam had to be crossed. The snow made it impossible to know where to step. I poked my hiking poles through the snow to test the footing, but I still stepped blindly. About midway across, my foot plunged through the snow and got stuck between the sticks that cemented the dam together. My body had already propelled forward for the next step, but my stuck foot couldn't follow. I kinda sorta fell. Not a BAM-you're-on-the-ground fall, but a slow motion oh-shit-I'm-going-down fall. I landed on my knee in snow-covered mud. Crap. Not only did I have wet, muddy feet, I had wet, muddy pants.

At least the beaver dam meant I was close to Fiona. I came to the sign for the spur trail that led to the dead-end road and plodded up the trail with my muddy feet and knee, hobbling to Fiona. I started her up for heat, peeled off my wet boots and placed them under the heater vent on the passenger side. What about dinner? I could eat here, I thought, but I'd like to have cell service to Facetime one of the kids for company. Now that I was spending more nights on the trail versus day trips, I often "made the rounds" if I had service, tapping the name of one of the five kids on my phone just seeing who was around to chat. I drove until bars appeared on my phone and pulled over to eat.

Three emails from Mitch that day. Though I had been silent for six weeks since he screamed at me in my front yard,

SQUATTER

I blamed myself for his continued contact. Somewhere along the way in life, I learned and accepted that I was responsible when people treated me badly. Now it was time to make my intentions clear. In writing.

Your emails are intrusive in my life and they need to stop.
Send.

13

The addiction is real and I'm not feeling so great.

Murphy Flowage campground was deserted and quiet. I set up my tent between patches of snow. About a half-an-hour of light remained until sunset. No beautiful colors that evening. The snowy day's gloom would turn to night without fanfare. With no cell service and darkness minutes away, there was nothing to do but snuggle into my double sleeping bags and swipe through the days' photos.

A gunshot jolted me. My heart raced. The shot came from down the hill by the flowage. "Dang buddy–lights gettin' kinda low for hunting," I mumbled. After that, I simply stared at the dancing shadows on the tent ceiling created by bare tree branches and watched the light fade. And then it was dark in the Blue Hills of Wisconsin.

An owl hooted. A chipmunk scampered. Branches creaked in the wind. Acorns dropped from the trees; their high velocity created loud plunks as they hit the forest floor. But the sound that always made my eyes fly open and caused me to hold my breath was twigs snapping from unknown causes. My heart pounded as I lay frozen, hoping to be invisible to whatever was out there. I didn't want to be found. That's silly, I thought. There's nothing out there.

But maybe there is.

SQUATTER

Maybe a part of me wondered if aliens do swoop down from space to take people away. Or if Bigfoot really does roam our forests and tear posts to shreds. Maybe it watched me as I walked the trail. Or those lumberjacks really did see a Hodag near Rhinelander in the 1800s. The world was a vast place with creatures yet to be discovered. Who's to say we know of every life form that roams the wilderness…and beyond. So, I continued to lay still and quiet, because you really never know what's out there.

There were no monsters or aliens that night. But there were wolves. Their long, mournful howl carried through the forest, announcing to every creature that they ruled that wild place. I waited for sleep to come while Fiona stood guard a few yards away.

I awoke in the eighteen-degree morning darkness and sat up for a few minutes to acclimate to the cold air before dressing. After making breakfast in the dark, I drove back to the dead-end road to meet Fred. He would shuttle me in the opposite direction where I would finish all of the Blue Hills.

I told him about hearing the wolves.

"There are two wolf packs in the area and they each have their own territory," Fred said. "Murphy Flowage is near the boundary of the two packs."

Just outside of Weyerhaeuser, we passed an ordinary looking pole building. There was no sign to indicate what it might be. "That's a shrimp farm," Fred pointed out as we passed. I never would have guessed. I liked the few minutes spent with the shuttle drivers. Minutes to learn new things in new places.

Fred dropped me off at the trailhead as the sun rose above the distant trees on the horizon. I entered the snowy woods wearing my dry pair of boots. The other pair was still drying out on Fiona's floorboard. The heavy, gray clouds of late autumn stole the sun shortly after it appeared.

The trail led me across railroad tracks and farm fields lying dormant for the coming winter. I climbed over a fence stile, which allowed people to pass over while containing animals, and entered the county forest.

I had just scaled a ridge when my phone buzzed. Surprised that I had service, I pulled it out and saw it was Jory, my oldest son in Minnesota. I answered and kept walking, but the call dropped. We tried a couple more attempts, before realizing I had to stay on the snowy ridge to keep the signal.

"The Dallas Marathon is postponed until May," he said with disappointment. He was to run his first marathon in December and we had planned a family meetup to cheer him on in Dallas. Spending so much time on the trail made it easy to forget that Covid changed the world. Normally, I would have spent many of my free days in Minnesota. But we kept our distance during Covid which allowed me more time for the trail. I had been standing with my feet buried in the snow and shivered. We hung up, and I hiked along the ridge at the fastest pace I could to generate heat. My boots, again, became heavy and wet.

I stopped for lunch in a shelter of trees near Devil's Creek. Rocks, topped with tufts of white, dotted the creek's open water. Inches of undisturbed snow blanketed the creek's bridge. No one had been there since the prior day's snowfall. At that moment and in that place, the world belonged to me. I was in love with the trail and knew I'd be in a better place emotionally when I reached the end.

SQUATTER

* * *

With my wet socks tossed on Fiona's dash, I drove one county south. I pulled into Morris-Erickson County Park, along Long Lake, where I had stayed in September. The park was closed for the season. I rolled past the metal payment tube and chose a spot where I couldn't be seen from the road. After a dried lasagna dinner, I zipped myself in my sleeping bags and listened to a nature conversation. An owl in the tree above me hooted his solemn call. Then, from far across the lake, a reply echoed from a mystery caller. There was a long pause. Did my owl know the owl across the lake? Was he playing hard to get? Was he calling for a mate or was it a neighborly conversation? Maybe he was carefully formulating his response. He finally responded, and their conversation continued.

I lay in the cold darkness with one of the sleeping bags pulled over my head and checked my email. Mitch didn't acknowledge my message from yesterday. I didn't expect him to. Instead, he sent recordings of himself singing and wrote that he didn't want to be with anyone else. I took a deep breath. What do you do with someone like this? I thought. I didn't respond and tucked my phone away for the night. Sleep came beneath the haunting conversation between the owls.

* * *

At dawn, I drove down remote dirt roads to a parking area on the Firth Lake segment which would be my base for the day. Bike and hike one direction in the morning and then repeat in the other direction after lunch. Three pickup trucks sat in the gravel lot. Bow hunters was my guess for that early in the morning. I pulled on my humongous blaze-orange t-shirt over my puffy coat, donned my blaze-orange knit hat, and slipped on my thick mittens before pedaling off into the cold morning. The icy air bit my face, but the frozen dirt road made for easy pedaling.

    I locked up my bike at the trailhead and entered the snowy woods. The Ice Age Trail Guidebook described Firth Lake as having "high-relief hummocky topography." Google interpreted that to mean it's gonna be hilly. Despite the twenty-degree morning, sweat dripped down my chest as I navigated the hills. I stuffed my jacket in my pack and made sure to put back on the blaze-orange t-shirt.

    The trail led back to Fiona. I was right. A group of bow hunters stood around the other trucks. I approached, and they smiled and nodded with a look of surprise. Maybe they didn't expect Fiona to belong to a solo female hiker.

    After lunch, I buzzed over to retrieve my bike. When I returned, the hunters were gone. I started my second shuttle of the day down 250th Avenue as the temperature hovered near freezing. The dirt road had thawed to a soft mush making pedaling more challenging. Something caught my eye up ahead. I braked hard and the wet brakes squealed in rebellion. A black bear emerged from the woods. I stood in awe as he lumbered across the road, far enough away to be unconcerned about my presence. My second bear encounter. But the first one I had actually witnessed in real time.

    I passed the five-hundred-mile mark in the misty woods containing beautiful tamarack trees. In addition to seeing the bear, the day's reward was crossing an impressive five-hundred-foot boardwalk that spanned over an old beaver dam. Five hundred for five hundred.

SQUATTER

* * *

Two long connecting road walks were all that remained for me to finish the North. Nearly sixteen miles in one county and twenty-six miles in another. I pored over the map to find a way to shorten the twenty-six mile one. I couldn't walk that in one day, and I didn't want to drag it out over two. The suggested route avoided busy State Highway 64. But walking it would shave off seven miles. I could take 64 then turn onto a quiet county highway for the last few miles to the Otter Lake Bait Shop. A total of eighteen miles. Doable. I'd be crabby and hurting, but it would get finished. Next, the shuttle plan. Walking on Highway 64 was one thing. I'd face traffic and be able to step down into the ditch when semis passed. But there's no way I was riding my bike on Highway 64. That was a ticket to be airlifted to a trauma unit.

Liz was my answer. Anna had gone back to Minneapolis leaving Liz as the only other driver at home. It was seventy-five miles away. That would be the longest distance I would ask her to shuttle. She agreed, and the plan was a go.

Until morning rolled around. Six am in late October was very different from a summer six am. Birds didn't chirp to a brightening sky offering the promise of soon to arrive sun. Six am in late October was still the middle of the night.

I started packing for the day and checked on Liz. Still in bed. No problem. She had always been responsible in getting up when she needed to. "Hey, Sweetheart…come on…it's time. I'm almost ready."

I finished packing my lunch and snacks. Wake up attempt number two. "Hey, Liz…come on…it's time…I gotta get goin'," I said with a bit of edge to my voice.

Wake up attempt number three. "Hey Liz!" I pounded on the lump in the bed. "I'm ready! Let's go!"

A muffled voice rose from the lump. "It's too early."

I pulled out the mean mom card. "Dang it...get up NOW! We're going to Chippewa County!"

* * *

After Liz dropped me off for the road walk at the end of the Chippewa River segment, I walked across the blue metal bridge into the town of Cornell. We left Fiona parked at Otter Lake Bait. She gave a stiff wave. I felt kinda bad. But I had to be here. I had recently started taking Aleve before longer days instead of afterwards. And that morning I forgot. I kept the bottle in Fiona's center console to help remind me, but I still forgot. A long, dark, gray, painful day loomed before me.

As I walked down 64, I stopped at every guard rail to stretch. Then I moved to squatting when traffic cleared, knowing that an approaching vehicle would mistake me for a roadside pooper. After four hours on Highway 64, I turned onto a county highway for another two hours. "Oh my gosh...where is it?" I groaned, hoping Otter Lake Bait would appear after rounding a turn or cresting a hill. My gait had become that weird, hip-twisting waddle. I refused to look at Guthook to check the distance. I didn't want to be disappointed. My hopes had been continuously dashed after rounding multiple curves to only be greeted by more trees and fields. I finally had to look. One more freakin' mile. No matter what the day's distance, the last mile was always torture. And then I saw it!

The sign with the green fish: *Otter Lake Bait–Gas–Ice–Groceries–Celebrating 21 Years*. What a thing of beauty. Fiona sat waiting with Aleve. I changed into my Crocs, popped

SQUATTER

the pain reliever and limped into the store where Laura and I had eaten pizza last summer. I wandered the two aisles. I wanted to buy something more than a candy bar in return for their generosity in allowing me to park there all day. Jars of locally made maple syrup lined a shelf. I took one to the counter. The first of many maple syrup jars I would buy as a thank you, as I completed the trail.

* * *

November 4, 2020 was the third anniversary of our first date. After running errands, I pulled into my driveway. A paper grocery bag sat by the side door. Inside was a candle, stationary, coffee, chocolate, and a card. I left it outside and grabbed my phone to look at my spam email.

3:53 pm. *Not sure if you're home. Left a gift at your side door.*

3:55 pm. *Hoping to see you even for a few minutes. Today is a special anniversary for me.*

4:10 pm. *I'm parked a few blocks away if you decide that I can say hi on the anniversary of the day we met three years ago.*

While making supper, Mitch's face peered through the kitchen door, startling me. I opened the door a few inches, but didn't offer a greeting.

"Did you look at what's in the bag?" Mitch asked in a forlorn tone, glancing down at his gift.

"I did and I can't accept it. It's over Mitch," I said. "You need to move on."

"I can't," Mitch mumbled with tears in his eyes. "I can't move on. Please…can I have a hug…please?"

I wanted that hug. I wanted to love him. But it just couldn't be. I shook my head and gently closed and locked the door.

He stood there for a while and then drove away, leaving the gifts behind.

Yolanda DeLoach

I woke up at four-thirty the next morning to get ready for my final day in the North. Mitch had continued to send emails until 2:00 am. I put the bag in the garage.

* * *

I unloaded my bike and began pedaling the sixteen miles to the Rusk/Chippewa county line. After an hour-and-a-half, I reached the county sign that I previously locked my bike to when coming from the opposite direction. For some reason, I had taken my bike lock off at home and forgot it. I pushed my bike through the ditch's tall grass, up a hill into the woods and hid it under some branches.

I started the walk back to Fiona with my eye on the prize of finishing the North. The county highway stretched before me, slicing through brown fields that spanned the horizon to meet a rare, blue November sky. Far up ahead, a semi-truck sat at the side of the road near a farm. Maybe waiting to load grain or corn. The truck was a mere speck in the distance. Something to focus on. Sort of like keeping your eye on mountains looming on the horizon. They look like they're just ahead, but they're really forever away.

The miles dragged on after passing the truck and eventually, the green water tower of Weyerhaeuser came into view, looking like a giant, upside-down bulb syringe. A nose sucker is what I called it when the kids were little. I crossed the railroad tracks and headed out of town. I reached Fiona and took my routine end-of-hike selfie, to timestamp and organize my photos, when a pickup truck burned up the road toward me. The driver slammed to a stop and rolled down the window. A dirty, gruff looking man with a long, unkept beard glared at me.

"Are ya just a hiker?" he demanded. I didn't like his tone.

SQUATTER

"Yeaahh..." I cautiously answered, I guessed the hiking boots, backpack, and trekking poles along with the prominent Ice Age Trail sign weren't much of a clue.

"This yer vehicle?" He gestured to Fiona. Was I parked wrong? I took a quick glance to make sure her tires were off the asphalt. They were. I almost answered him like an obedient child. "Whataya doin' here?" he insisted.

I didn't owe him an explanation. Unease gripped my stomach. Ignoring his questions, I marched toward Fiona while frantically unzipping my pack for the keys. To be seen better on road walks, I wore my huge, blaze-orange t-shirt. Maybe he thought I had been hunting on private land. Maybe the land next to the trail was his.

Too bad.

I was a legally parked hiker at the Southern Blue Hills trailhead and had every right to be there. If he wanted to inquire about what I was up to or if Fiona was mine, he could have asked in a more approachable tone. I was fucking over being nice to men who behaved badly. He glared at me for a few moments before doing a Y-turn and spun away at a roaring speed. I tossed my stuff into Fiona and took off, not bothering to change into my Crocs until I got into Weyerhaeuser.

I soon forgot about the crabby, wild-looking man and pumped up the music for the ride home. I had completed the North. Well over six hundred miles from the Western Terminus through the county south of home. All before gun deer season. Two goals completed. Not seeing Mitch in nearly two months—goal in progress. I know, I know, I'd gone a couple of months without seeing him before. But this time was different. This time, I had the trail.

And the trail was magic.

Algoma

My bike

Marathon County

Porcupine and bear

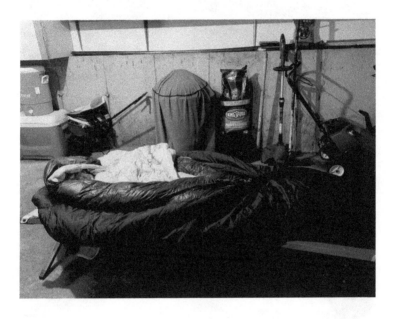

Laura's garage

Beaver dam, Rusk County

Private land

Winter road walk

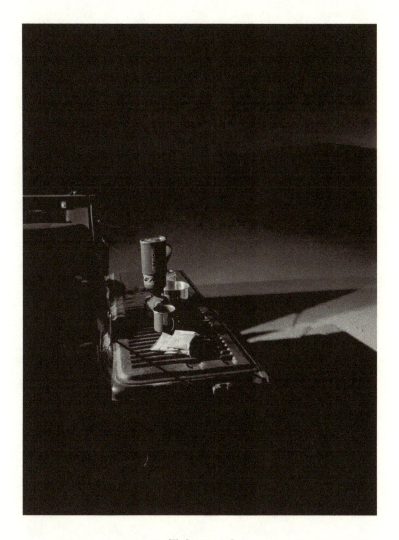

Tailgate meal

Fiona and me

14

I'm in the southern portion of the state now.
I'm trying to like it. I really am.

I felt a bit bummed after finishing the North. The rugged, wild, and isolated part of the trail. I loved its overgrown footpaths and being alone in the woods. I could recall the specific instances of meeting other people because it had been so rare.

Instead of making comparisons, I made a mental note to enjoy what the rest of the trail had to offer. Two things would be a challenge when heading south. I had been dropping my pants willy-nilly whenever I had to pee. Free-range bathroom breaks would have to be more strategic. And camping was going to be an issue. Vehicle break-ins also concerned me. Windows had been smashed at trailheads throughout the southern portion of the state. I always left my purse hidden and locked in Fiona. But now, I decided I'd carry my wallet while hiking and leave Fiona unlocked. My hope was that someone would open the door to rummage through my stuff instead of smashing the window. I figured thieves weren't after camping equipment.

I pulled out of the driveway on a dark, early November morning and headed to Green County. I figured if I was heading south, I might as well go all the way to the bottom. Green County bordered Illinois. The bottom of the trail's U.

My plan was to move north to close the gap before moving toward the Eastern Terminus.

On the drive, I repeatedly played two songs. "Welcome Home" by Radical Face and "We're Going Home" by Vance Joy. I liked the idea of home representing a solid me. I looked forward to the new person that waited for me at the end of the trail. A new me. I didn't know exactly how that would look. But a shift was happening.

* * *

The next couple of days would be along rail/trail and roads. That day would be the Monticello Segment. Rail/trails weren't my hiking favorite, but they made bike shuttling easier (except for the monstrous Tuscobia shuttle). There's no studying the map for a suitable road route, just zip down the old railroad grade and walk back.

But that day, I had the brilliant idea to shorten my rail/trail bike shuttle. I don't know why I thought a mere six-and-a-half miles needed to be shortened. I pedaled the suggested road route until outside of the little town of Dayton, where I veered off onto a county highway, well before the rail/trail entrance. I would piece my way down to Monticello on back roads. Gosh, I'm clever. I smiled to myself.

There's a reason the railroad chose the routes they did. Sure, railroad companies blasted and moved earth to make a flatter grade, but only after choosing the path of least resistance. Why I thought I would find a better route to Monticello than the railroad surveyors was a question I asked myself. Well, I didn't really ask myself that. I just swore a lot.

I pedaled into relentless wind. Its resistance held me back from going full speed down hills. At times, walking would have been faster than pedaling. My wheels navigated through invisible sludge. One hill after another. After an hour and twenty minutes of hills, wind, and misery, I arrived in Monticello. The vintage red train depot at the trailhead welcomed me, as it once did for the weary train travelers of a bygone era. I locked up my bike and noticed the pit toilets. Score. My first segment outside of the Northwoods started off in luxury.

I returned to Fiona in the early afternoon. The glorious sun shone unseasonably warm. There was plenty of time left for another bike/hike. But after getting up at three-thirty and dealing with the bike shuttle fiasco, I was done. Time to figure out where to spend the night. Even though it was off-season for camping and Covid, I drove over to New Glarus Woods State Park. As expected, the office was closed but the gates were open. I picked a spot, set up my tent, and attempted to read for the rest of the afternoon.

I had been an avid reader and for years kept a reading list. The list came to a halt after meeting Mitch. Only one book in 2018 and one in 2019. I had to fight for the time to read those two books. Mitch monopolized every moment of my free time and acted like a spoiled kid if I did something for myself. I initially thought his behavior was due to the excitement of a new relationship. But something sinister hid behind his actions. He snuffed out my interests, almost stripping me of my individuality. Sometimes I felt like nothing more than his pet. As time with Mitch went on, anxiety and turmoil had stolen my concentration for reading. That afternoon at my campsite, I read sporadically, but still struggled to concentrate. Healing takes time. I tried not to worry about it.

The November day had been summer-like, but a four-forty-five sunset jolted me back to reality. Zero chance of rain, so no rainfly over the tent. I stretched out and looked up at the sky. Even though I was in the woods, the sky told me that civilization was nearby. Planes bound for Madison, Milwaukee, and Chicago repeatedly flew overhead. To the north, the sky lit up with Madison's glow. Few twinkling stars would call to me that night. But, I was grateful for the stars that were out. What a treat it was to lay in my tent and gaze up at the night sky during a Wisconsin November.

I was up at five and headed to the trailhead for a tailgate breakfast under the Morning Star. The day would be along rail/trail into the town of Albany. I did not search for an alternate bike shuttle route. I pedaled down the crushed gravel trail with ease. The day, again, promised to be in the seventies, but the early morning air rushed past me with a November chill. Twilight created a softness to the world. Ghostly patches of fog clung to low-lying open areas, while the sun rose through the bare trees. Soon I coasted into Albany.

The town was coming alive for the day. Dog walkers, runners, and those strolling along nodded as I rode by. A pajama-clad lady holding a steaming cup of coffee waved a greeting from her backyard. I locked up my bike and started my return hike. Outside of Albany, the old railroad bed stretched before me. Up ahead, a white-haired gentleman walked with a cane, stopping every so often to gaze into the woods. I imagined he gleaned wisdom from those woods that the rest of us couldn't see. I quickly gained on him. He was smartly dressed in a tweed jacket. Sensing my presence, he turned to me. He held a pipe to his mouth. Not just any ol' pipe, but a cool Sherlock Holmes one. He looked like someone who had the answers to life's questions.

"Good morning, young lady," he greeted me as I passed. "You're definitely on the right path to enjoy this beautiful day."

The right path. That grandfatherly gentleman said I was on the right path. I imagined we could have a conversation in front of a fireplace. I'd tell him I'm such an idiot. I'd say I was a fool. He would listen without judgment, giving an understanding nod while puffing on his pipe. He would say, "There's nothing wrong with you." I would let that sink in. That's not the message I've received throughout my life.

I wrapped up our imaginary chat, wished him a great day, and continued down the right path. I moved at a fast clip before jumping at the sight of a good-sized snake crossing the trail. Some believe that a snake crossing your path means that a new phase of your life is emerging. I glanced back down the straightaway. The old man with the cool pipe was gone.

The red Monticello train station came into view. I had been feeling short on calories the last few trips out. My metabolism churned through calories faster than I could replace them.

I drove into Albany and was leery about hitting up a diner near noon, thinking about the lunch crowd. I peeked through the diner's window. Only one person, so I went in and sat at the counter. The maskless waitress greeted me. She stood face-to-face with me across the narrow counter. I instinctively leaned back. Covid numbers were rising, and I wasn't about to let anything keep me off the trail. After ordering, I snatched up my phone and Googled Covid numbers for Green County. I devoured my second breakfast that cost a whopping $6.33. I left a good tip and stepped out into the unusually warm November afternoon.

SQUATTER

I pedaled a few miles for a road walk. I had never been someone who listened to things while walking. But the situation with Mitch had me hungry for knowledge. I wanted to learn about toxic relationships and my part in it. Road walking would become my podcast time.

Back at New Glarus Woods, it would be a second gorgeous night without the rainfly. I awoke in the night to the yelping of coyotes. They weren't near enough to cause concern. Plus, Fiona faithfully waited in the moonlight to shelter me if need be. I unzipped the tent and crawled out to pee. There was a time I would have been too spooked to step out into the dark woods. Now it felt like home. Healing is kinda like that. There often isn't a specific moment of healing, but one day you realize you aren't afraid of something anymore. Or that you can do something you couldn't do before. Or you think differently about something. Healing is a process.

The next morning, I began the trail in Dane County, the county of the state's capital. I had the luxury of a shuttle ride from a trail angel named Greg. He met me at the southern trailhead of the Verona segment. Even with a mask, I could tell he greeted me with a smile. We chatted about Covid.

"My wife works in healthcare, too. Things are just crazy," he said. I thought about our own hospital and areas that had been converted to Covid units. I had worked on other units besides my own and cared for Covid patients. But mostly, I stayed in our small palliative care unit which felt a bit sheltered from the craziness.

We drove through the countryside that was a mix of farms and housing developments. A classic farm would be on one side of the road and the other would be a cluster of earth-toned homes perched on manicured lawns. I told Greg about the coyotes.

"I was surprised to hear them so near populated areas," I said.

"Oh, they thrive around here. Easy food. No predators. Yeah, they're near cities," Greg said. We pulled into the trailhead.

I waved goodbye to Greg and headed into the woods of the Brooklyn Wildlife segment, the first actual foot path I'd do of the southern portion. I walked through the meadows, prairies and clusters of woods all clothed in November brown. Another seventy-degree day would hold off an inevitable upper-Midwestern winter.

Once again, I had forgotten to take an Aleve that morning. Along a road walk, the beauty of happy red barns against the blue sky helped keep my mind off the pain. The farms in southern Wisconsin tended to be well maintained and picturesque. I turned onto County Road PB, anticipating an easy final mile.

County Road PB must have been a major thoroughfare for that area. A string of semis and cars backlogged behind the slowest driver approached me. I stepped off the shoulder and into the grass to keep from getting blown away and nearly stepped on a mangled deer carcass. I stepped around it, avoiding the frozen look on its face, as vehicles roared by. The next line of cars and semis snaked its way toward me. Another deer that had met its unfortunate end lay in the grass. The turbulent wake of Freightliners and Peterbilts forced me to keep walking through the grass. High speed traffic on my right. Pain in my legs. Dead deer on my left. I passed a dozen deer carcasses in that last mile to the Verona trailhead.

So that was Dane County. The Land of Abundant Roadkill.

SQUATTER

* * *

At home I flipped through the mail. Tucked in between shopping flyers and credit card offers was a postcard from Mitch. *It makes me incredibly sad that you would wonder if I ever lied about my faithfulness to you. Be safe.*

None of the podcasts I'd listened to gave advice on how to deal with that.

15

I slept my first night in a garage.

The previous week's remarkable weather was a distant memory. Now, the blustery mid-November skies warned of the coming winter. Camping at New Glarus Woods wouldn't be practical now that I had moved farther into Dane County. While hiking with Laura last summer, she offered her guest room or yard for tenting when I made it down her way. Staying in her home wasn't an option due to Covid and my cat allergy. We texted a plan to set up my tent in her yard. *You can use the utility room toilet just off the garage.* I worried about the garage door rumbling at night during a potty run and disturbing her. *Could I just sleep in the garage?* I texted. A camping cot would be perfect to keep me off of the cold cement. She agreed that it was a good idea.

Before dawn, I packed and got ready to leave for the two-hour drive back to Dane County. All I needed was to load my bike. I pulled the tailgate handle but it wouldn't open. The tonneau cover had frozen to the top of the tailgate. What good is a cover if you can't open it in cold weather?

"Dammit!" I mumbled in frustration, while giving the latch a few more tugs. I Googled a solution. Someone said to pour hot water on it. I heated up some water.

No go.

SQUATTER

Someone else said to use a hair dryer. I rummaged through the basement for an extension cord and then stood in the driveway blow-drying Fiona's behind.

No go.

I stomped into the kitchen and yanked out the dryer cord from the wall with a frustrated sigh of resignation. I'd have to lose hours waiting for the sun to melt the grip on the cover.

I missed Mitch at that moment. If he were here, the scene would be different. I would have discovered the frozen tailgate, shrugged my shoulders and walked back into the house to tell Mitch. Then, I'd enjoy a cup of coffee while the problem would have been solved by the Fixer of All Things. But I didn't have a Fixer of All Things anymore. Maybe Bonnie Tyler was right. I needed a hero.

An idea dropped into my head. The car wash! Kwik Trip was a few blocks away. I jumped into Fiona and in a few moments, we were cruising through the wash. Nearing the wash's end, a jolt and bang let me know that the tailgate came down. "Whoo Hoo! Yes!" I hollered, and sped home. Maybe I could be the hero of my story.

I loaded up my bike and ran back inside for a water bottle. I should bring a gift to Laura for her generous offer. Of course, that would come to mind the moment I needed to leave. Why was I such a dunderhead when it came to those kinds of social graces? Shoot. The unopened bottle of maple syrup from Otter Lake Bait sat on the counter. Everyone likes maple syrup, right? And if they don't, they know someone who does. Perfect. I grabbed the bottle, backed out of the driveway and drove down the interstate to Dane County.

The days heading into winter would be a race against the sun to finish the miles before a four-thirty sunset. I wouldn't always win. In the darkness on a bluff overlooking the city of Cross Plains, I pulled on my headlamp. Festive lights twinkled in the neighborhood below. Homes emitted a warm holiday glow. In November, our world shrinks and life becomes smaller. We close up and prepare for the coming long winter. Life looked cozy and magical from up on the bluff. I stealthily moved through the dark. An outsider looking in on a charmed world. After making my way down the bluff, I emerged from the trail in a backyard and walked the blocks to where Fiona waited. I made the half-hour drive to Laura's while listening to the NPR voices report on the presidential election results and Covid.

I pulled into Laura's garage. We greeted each other wearing masks, and I handed her the maple syrup.

"Oh nice! Thanks!" she said. "I'll eat dinner out here with you. Wanna burrito?" she asked. I had my own food, but I accepted her offer.

Covid had been raging through both of our workplaces. We sat socially distanced in lawn chairs, wearing our winter coats and ate burritos. Due to the cat, I couldn't hang out inside.

I set up the cot and snuggled in for the night next to a snowblower, a weed wacker, rakes, a shovel, and a bag of Kingsford charcoal. I was going to spend the night in a cold garage, during a global pandemic while solo hiking the Ice Age Trail to break free from an ex-fiancé who claimed our relationship was blessed by God. Some things you just can't make up.

I left Laura's garage in the morning darkness and picked up a McDonald's breakfast sandwich. I felt short on calories again and would need the greasy sandwich for the seventeen-mile day plus bike shuttling. I remembered my Aleve while in the drive-thru.

SQUATTER

The night before, while snuggled in my sleeping bags, I pored over Google Maps looking for a decent bike route. I needed to go north, but going directly north would cross busy intersections. Going a mile south would add distance, but would take me through the quiet neighborhoods of Verona.

Either direction, the shuttle would start on the Nightmare Highway of Deer Carcasses: County Road PB. Packing up the last of my stuff, I debated which gloves to grab: the warm, puffy ones or the thin, lightweight ones. The twenty-degree morning would give way to a forty-degree day. "Eh…I don't need the puffy ones today," I mumbled to myself and closed Fiona's door.

I pulled the blaze-orange t-shirt over my coat to be better seen on the road and clipped on my helmet. I waited for a break in traffic and zoomed off. Only one mile. Come on, get movin', I urged myself on and glanced over my shoulder. A line of roaring vehicles fast approached. My turn-off was in sight. I frantically pedaled my ancient, heavy Schwinn as fast as my fifty-two-year-old legs could make it go. I skidded around the corner onto the side road, kicking up gravel dust like a hot shot as semis blew past.

After the stress of the nightmarish highway subsided, the freezing pain in my hands grabbed my attention as the wind cut through my thin gloves. I stopped, pulled off the gloves and held my red, raw fingers against the back of my warm neck. Soon they would painfully throb and turn white. I have Raynaud's Syndrome, where my fingers' blood vessels overreact to cold and become too constricted, turning them white. I regretted leaving the puffy mittens with Fiona. I would be on my bike for at least one painful, miserable hour. I curled up my fingers inside the gloves hoping that would help. The throbbing turned to numbness. What I really wanted was to stop and shove my hands down my pants next to my body warmth. But standing on Main Street, USA with your hands down your pants while school buses roll by is what weirdos do. And that's a good way to end up in jail.

I couldn't take the pain any longer and at the edge of town, turned into a Casey's convenience store. I put on my mask and flew into the restroom, running my hands under lukewarm water. Sweet relief. I bought hot chocolate and a cheap fruit pie. Masks were required, but the clerk said I could eat in a corner before biking on. I set my treats on a stack of soda cases and stood far from the other customers. My stiff fingers thawed around the hot chocolate. An hour-and-a-half after leaving Fiona, I finally arrived at the Madison trailhead. It had been a miserable morning brought on by my own foolishness.

The day would test my open-mindedness about the trail. I passed through a golf course, over four-lane highways and suburban developments where a sea of sameness and conformity stretched to the horizon. Despite human development, two deer peered at me through the trees near the golf course. The trail made no claims to be total wilderness. It highlighted both urban and wild areas of Wisconsin. I intended to find joy in both.

The Aleve I remembered to take in the morning did its job. I would have another hour on my bike to Old Sauk Pass for my second bike shuttle of the day. The November afternoon sun hung low in the sky. I walked south through the Ice Age Reserve Wildlife Area. A bowhunter walked ahead of me through an open field of dried prairie grasses. He settled in at the tree line. The shadows grew long and daylight dimmed. I was thankful for my blaze-orange shirt and hat as I wondered how many hunters might be watching from the trees, waiting for me to cross the field.

I entered the Valley View segment alongside private property just before sunset. Valley View wound through the upper-crust world of Dane County suburbia. Not cookie-cutter suburban homes, but grand, countryside mansions. I'd lived in the same 1920s one-and-a-half story, eleven-hundred-square-foot house for over twenty-five years. What does one do with all that space?

I reached the prairie portion of the segment as the sun went down. A brown horizon met clouds soaked with purples and reds. I put on my headlamp. Darkness set in and the trail led through more neighborhoods. I again returned to being an outsider in the dark, privy to fleeting moments in the lives of strangers. Homey, secure moments illuminated by the magical glow right out of a Thomas Kinkade painting. At least, that's what I imagined. Because we never know what life is truly like behind closed doors. No matter how warm the glow.

* * *

Back at Laura's garage we sat in our winter coats and shared a rotisserie chicken that I had picked up. I took a second Aleve and slipped into my sleeping bag after eating. My nest until five the next morning. My body needed eleven hours of rest. There had been nights when my bones throbbed so badly that I had trouble falling asleep. I'd gotten better at remembering to take a pain reliever before the day started. I fell asleep next to Fiona, who stood silhouetted by the streetlight shining in through the garage window.

Morning quickly rolled around. Laura's garage must have been somewhat heated. The outside temperature was twenty but my water bottle didn't freeze in the night. But the garage air was still mighty nippy as I dressed for the day. I drove back to the Ice Age Reserve Wildlife Area. I'd be going in the opposite direction than the prior evening to finish up Cross Plains.

The morning turned windy after the sun rose. The wind at my back while I pedaled pushed me to the edge of town. I remembered to wear the big, puffy mittens. I faced the wind on the return walk. The strong gusts lifted my braids. I pressed into the wind to keep my momentum moving forward. I had a short break from the gusts while passing a quaint farm tucked alongside a steep hill. I gazed at the charming, tan stone house. Farmhouses weren't made like that in my area of the state. The road passed intimately close to the tidy farmyard. I imagined that over a century ago a wagon or buggy would have ridden up on a simple dirt path worn in the grass. I left the shelter of the hillside and a gust of wind pitted my face with road grit.

The second shuttle of the morning took me into Cross Plains. On the bike shuttle into town, I stopped at an historical marker that told the story of Haney's Tavern. The tavern was one of Dane County's oldest existing buildings and had been owned by a guy named Berry Haney. Inside his tavern, Haney shot a man. Being the stand-up guy that he was, Haney nursed the man back to health. Haney ended up deserting his wife and moving to Kansas. He settled on a Kansas farm with a third wife. The sign specifically read A third wife and not HIS third wife. I think that meant he was married to more than one woman at a time. In 1858, he was shot to death. The sign didn't say who shot him. Maybe it was the deserted wife. You play stupid games; you win stupid prizes.

SQUATTER

Cross Plains was home to the Ice Age Trail headquarters. Hikers were encouraged to stop in and chat. But with Covid, they were closed to the public. All I could do was take a picture of the giant, metal woolly mammoth (the trail's mascot) in their gardens and keep battling the wind. I finally made it back to Fiona.

I opened the door and plopped into the driver's seat. My heavy body couldn't move another inch. My face stung from windburn after powering through gusts all day. I had done two bike shuttles and only walked twelve miles. I was hoping for a seventeen or eighteen-mile day. The low-hanging sun announced that daylight would soon be gone. I dug into my jacket pocket for my phone. Four o'clock. I could get another bike and hike done on a road walk in the dark. I stared at the prairie's brown grasses rippling in the wind. The nine-day gun deer season was coming up, and I wouldn't be hiking during that time. I wanted to push on for more miles but my body couldn't go any farther. Sometimes you just have to surrender.

Take me home, Fiona.

16

"Never Encourage anyone to become a lawyer,"
says Life's Little Instruction Book.
Heck, I'd add, "never encourage anyone to date one."
But then again, I'm a little tainted right now.

During my hiking break for gun deer season, a flower delivery van pulled into my driveway. The driver presented me with a vase of red roses surrounding one white rose. The card read, *Always so beautiful. Mitch.* I wasn't surprised. Three years ago, we started our physical relationship. I closed the door and stood a moment holding the flowers. What do I do with these? I didn't want to display them, but throwing them away seemed wasteful. I had thrown away the grocery-store flowers he left over my backyard fence. I felt a little guilty for placing more value on the roses versus the Plain Jane flowers. I put them in my bedroom for the time being. I'd be back on the trail soon and wouldn't have to look at them. Mitch inquired in an email if I received the flowers. I went to bed that night without responding.

In the morning, I decided to be nice and at least reply: *Yes, I got them. But please don't send me more stuff, k?* I intentionally didn't thank him. Why did I feel the need to be nice? Be. Nice. Where was that coming from?

SQUATTER

* * *

In the darkness of an early December morning, I headed south on the interstate. Exactly three months had passed since I'd left Mitch's house for the last time. His daily emails continued. Even if I ignored my spam email, just knowing they were there weighed on me. I felt encouraged. The "hit" I had been feeling when seeing his name had faded. That had to mean the trail was working its magic. I was breaking the addiction. But having him lurk at the edge of my life made me anxious. How could I move on when he wouldn't let go?

The trail provided an answer. As long as I continued along the trail, I would stay on my new path forward.

This trip out, I'd continue moving north. It was a Thursday, and if I went in segment order, that would put me at Devil's Lake State Park over the weekend. Wisconsin's most popular state park. Not a place I wanted to be on a weekend. And the next few days were forecasted to be sunny, with highs in the upper thirties. Gorgeous weather in early December would bring out the masses.

I'd only been to Devil's Lake once. About twenty-five years ago, I popped in on a drive back from Madison. Being from the northern half of Wisconsin, it didn't occur to me to visit the state's populated southern half to enjoy the outdoors. I headed farther north. The Upper Peninsula of Michigan and Lake Superior acted as giant magnets.

I made a tactical move to hit the nearly eleven-mile Devil's Lake segment on the drive down. The segment almost created a loop. Both trailheads were on the same road, one mile apart. I pulled into the first trailhead I came to. The northern one. I admit that I'm not one who did intense planning for my hikes. I winged a lot of things. Well actually, most things. Many hikers were smart planners: inquiring in the Facebook group about wind direction, hills, and which direction was best for biking. I did not. My mind was so focused on the mess with Mitch, that I didn't care what difficulties the trail brought. Nothing the trail could throw at me could match the stress of my current situation. I admit that the lack of detailed planning cost me at times. But my Devil's Lake bike shuttle would not be one of those times.

I sailed the mile down the county highway. Even with my neck gaiter pulled over my nose and mouth, the icy air's sting made my eyes water. "Woohoooooo…" I yelled as my neck gaiter blew down, and winter tears streaked my face. I relished in the exhilarating, pedal-free ride that came about by sheer luck.

My decision to hike Devil's Lake on a December weekday morning paid off as I only encountered three people. I carefully descended the steep stones of the nearly vertical East Bluff. Again, luck was with me in that I chose the direction that wasn't climbing up. I stepped aside for a man with a middle-aged protruding belly in workout attire panting as he ascended the rocky cliff.

The more gradual climb to the West Bluff was not nearly as dramatic as the East. The temperature rose above freezing. I shed my winter jacket and hiked in my hoodie. The view of Devil's Lake from the five-hundred-foot bluff was what people flocked to see. The deep blue lake spanned below me from the bluff. I sat on a boulder, pulled out a fig bar and Facetimed Grace to show her the view. After striking a selfie pose hinting at a coolness and youthfulness that I didn't possess, I continued on.

I picked up my bike at the trailhead a mile down the road and thought I'd check out camping options for when I'd be back this way in a few days. Laura's garage in Dane

County would soon be too far to be a reasonable option. I drove into the state park to check it out.

Ranger stations around the state were closed for Covid. That's what I was hoping for at Devil's Lake. I could pitch my tent at sunset and be gone well before sunrise. I'd become good at being a stealth squatter. But no. With Devil's Lake being so popular, the station was open. I pulled up to the window with my credit card ready to purchase next year's park sticker. A masked ranger greeted me and handed me park information.

"We're open all year for camping," she said.

"Great," I said. Maybe it would be an okay choice.

I pulled into a parking space and looked at the information. Thirty-five dollars! To pitch a tent. In the winter. To be here for less than twelve hours? No way. Even though I made my own money and most of the kids were financially on their own, decades of raising a large family on a truck driver's income made it hard to let go of the being-tight-with-money mindset.

I cruised around the park. It would be impossible to squat here and not be seen. I pulled out my phone and zoomed in on Google Maps looking for anything…a nature preserve…a quiet dead-end road…something. I drove by the Sauk Prairie Recreation Area. Nothing. If I was on foot, I could squat easily. But hiding a truck wouldn't be easy. Fiona would give us away. How would I continue the trail once I got too far from Laura's? Hotels were not an option that would fit my budget. I sighed and shook my head. Damn it.

I drove into Merrimac on my way to Laura's and waited in line for the car ferry that would take me across the Wisconsin River. I had taken the ferry many times over the years as a scenic detour either to or from Madison. The Merrimac

Ferry's long history began in 1844, as a human-powered ferry service to carry wagon teams across the river. Historical accounts are conflicted on how much the crossing cost. Some say thirty-five cents. Others say a dollar. A gasoline engine was added around the turn of the century. In 1933, the ferry became part of Wisconsin's State Highway System. A free ferry operated by the county. The ferry was part of the trail route and usually closed by the end of November when ice began forming. Winter hikers had to detour around. The unusual December warm spell kept the ice at bay. I pulled onto the ferry for the seven-minute ride as streaks of pink stretched across the sky.

I picked up a pizza to share with Laura in her garage. The aroma of warm cheese and spicy sauce mingled with tools and trash bins.

"So many people at work have Covid," Laura said as she sat in her winter coat and opened the pizza box.

"Same," I replied. "I keep my distance from everyone…I am not getting sick." I ate until my belly was stuffed.

We said goodnight and I set up my cot. The cold winter nights had arrived, even if the days grew unseasonably warm. I added a blanket to my mass of bedding to stuff in between the sleeping bags. The garage had become my adventure home. I pulled my hoodie over my head, snuggled into my bag and posted the day's adventure in the Facebook group. I stewed about the cost of camping at Devil's Lake.

I'd just set my phone down for the night when it dinged the familiar Messenger notification. A couple from Illinois had read my post. They had land near Devil's Lake outside of Baraboo that they wanted to offer me for camping. *Could we give you a call?* Wow! Absolutely.

SQUATTER

"Because of your posts, we feel like we know you...plus with you being a nurse during this time, we wanted to help a sister out," Mike and Sandy said, and they gave me directions to their property. "If we had a way to get you a key, we'd offer you the house. You're welcome to sleep on the deck or anywhere on the property. There's a deer stand on the back end of the woods as well, if that sounds adventurous."

The call ended and I lay still for a moment, stunned by their generosity. Who does that? My own world and the greater world around me had become vile the last few years. Mike and Sandy's kind gesture offered hope to my cynical heart.

* * *

I backed out of Laura's garage just after five in the morning. The routine was to back out, walk in and close the garage door, then leave through the front door, locking it behind me. I drove to the trailhead while I ate a convenience store breakfast of yogurt, a banana, and coffee. I bobbed along to Dua Lipa before switching the station to NPR's Morning Edition.

The day would involve three bike shuttles, a couple of road walks and two-and-a-half trail segments. A piecemealing of sorts. I pulled into Indian Lake County Park. The morning star reflected on the lake and a sliver of light gray stretched across the eastern sky. I climbed into Fiona's bed to unload my bike by the light of the full moon. Despite the recent warm days, the icy morning clearly said it was December. My breath circled around me as I went through the familiar motions of unloading my heavy Schwinn. Climb into the bed. Stand up the bike. Step backward. Carefully watch each step. Climb down while balancing the bike in the bed. Keep my arms close to my body. Lift the bike down. I never got sloppy doing that.

I pedaled off into the predawn darkness. The sky had lightened as I passed the sign for Peter's Prairie. A swift movement to my left caught my eye. A glorious buck leaped out of the high grass and bounded across the road at full speed, on the verge of taking flight. I doubt he saw me.

That was not the first time a buck crossed my path while on a bike shuttle. Last summer, a buck, wearing his massive rack like a crown, sauntered out of the woods. He emerged at an angle, facing away from me. His regal vibe said, "Watch out ladies, I'm hot stuff." He was chill. He was king. And he didn't see me coming. I silently coasted down the hill, barreling toward him. When he finally sensed my approach, his dignified moment was ruined. He scrambled back into the woods like a clumsy drunk, crashing through the brush as I passed.

The sun peeked over the horizon when I locked my bike up at the trailhead next to the brown prairie, my ending spot prior to deer hunting. My 3.6-mile return walk turned into 4.6 miles. You'd think it would be easy to walk back the same way you just biked. But things looked different from the opposite direction. The road made a wonky slight turn that I missed. I should have consulted Guthook at the intersection, but I was too busy talking to myself and enjoying the sunrise. I didn't even catch my mistake as I passed a farm I didn't recognize. Hmmm…I don't remember that farm. I must have been really flying by, I mused. After reaching an intersection that I definitely didn't recognize. I pulled out my phone.

"Gosh darn it," I said. There was no shortcut to fix it other than returning to the wonky turn.

SQUATTER

About a quarter of a mile from Fiona, I came across papers scattered along the roadside. Pages from a book. *Life's Little Instruction Book.* Dozens of papers fluttered in the grass, as if they sprouted there, waiting to be picked by someone needing to glean their wisdom.

I bent down to pick up the pages. Both for the fun of reading them and to clean up the roadside. *Learn to play a musical instrument.* Oooo. I got that down. Piano and clarinet. Above average, but not great. My junior high band teacher convinced me to play the baritone saxophone in jazz band for a while. My skinny-kid-self felt clumsy and unattractive with the big instrument. Not cool looking like the alto sax players.

Don't leave a ring in the bathtub. Guilty. I had an old clawfoot tub. No possibility of making it into a shower since the ceiling slanted over it. My standards were a little low regarding the bathtub ring.

Be wary of people who tell you how honest they are. Whoa. I suppose that goes the same for how smart, educated, and superior one was as well. Numerous times Mitch had said that he wasn't like other people. *I am superior to others*, he once wrote.

I picked up all the pages, carried them back to Fiona and tucked them under the floor mat. After making a second breakfast of oatmeal, I grabbed my bike and headed up to Springfield Hill trailhead for another connecting route. During the road walk, I searched for podcasts about addiction in the abuse cycle.

I pedaled through my third bike shuttle and rode into the city of Lodi for the last portion of the day. Eastern Lodi Marsh and Lodi Marsh segments. Should be an easy-peasy afternoon, I thought. Since the segment names contained the word "marsh," I thought they'd be flat...you know... like a marsh. I followed the path into Eastern Lodi Marsh just outside of town. Soon I began a steep climb through the woods. My hiking poles hit the ground in a slow, steady rhythm up the hill. I naturally shifted to pursed lip breathing and my gait became a stiff waddle. I had already pedaled that damn heavy bike fourteen miles and walked twelve so far. I wasn't in the mood for surprise hills.

The Ice Age Trail Guidebook always sat nicely on Fiona's passenger seat. I recorded my hiking data in it: date, mileage, bike shuttle, or ride, where I slept, and any unusual weather. I had flipped through it when it first came and had used its maps before I bought Guthook. But I never actually read it. If I had, I would have learned that Eastern Lodi Marsh was rated a 4 out of 5 for hilliness and had "several dolomite ridges" and "incorporates outstanding views." Basically, the segment was full of rocky, steep hills high enough to offer views of the marsh. Not actually walking through the marsh.

Thank goodness, the following Lodi Marsh segment was lowland and marsh-like. Locals wandered the trail with kids and dogs. I wasn't used to sharing the trail with so many people. Who wouldn't want to be out on an unexpectedly gorgeous Friday evening in December? As the sun set, the temperature plunged, chilling me. I was damp with sweat from huffing it on the earlier hills. I slipped off my pack and pulled out my puffy jacket. Fiona waited a mile and a half away since there was no parking at the trailhead. I could barely move. I stretched a bit and then waddled along to the tapping rhythm of my hiking poles. My phone buzzed in my pocket. Chatting with my son, John, for a bit, kept my mind off of my discomfort. It took thirty minutes to walk that mile and a half. Fiona came into view as the last slice of orange surrendered to darkness. I had been on the move since before sun up. The simplicity of witnessing a day enter and leave while on the trail filled me with peace. Nothing needed to be accomplished but walking and biking.

Laura brought heated leftovers to the garage for dinner. "Since tomorrow's Saturday, I can shuttle you," she offered. I accepted. A day off from biking would be welcomed. I cleaned up a bit in her basement utility sink and took another Aleve before slipping into my nest of sleeping bags and blankets. Some nights my legs throbbed so badly I heard myself groaning in my sleep. I posted my day's thoughts in the Facebook group and then checked my spam email for what I knew waited there every day.

Northcentral Technical College was throwing away old traffic signs, so I grabbed them and left them on your retaining wall, Mitch wrote.

Years ago, when John was in high school, he and a friend were into "acquiring" street signs with interesting names. While he didn't respect and fully appreciate the taxpayer cost of replacing those signs, he at least drew the line at safety by not "collecting" stop or yield signs. Anyway…it's something we laugh about today. And something I shared with Mitch as some of those signs still hung in our basement.

Your behavior feels like stalking and it needs to stop, I wrote.

He responded, *I would like to meet you at a public place so I can talk to you? I'd appreciate that.*

Was it ever going to end? I felt I'd gone back to him too many times to win a restraining order. Plus, did I want to embarrass him in front of his peers? Why did I even care if he was embarrassed? For some reason, I did.

I did the only thing I knew to do at that moment. I kept moving on the trail.

17

Nature certainly makes me feel small at times.

I slept in until seven in Laura's garage. No one wants to get up at five on their day off to shuttle me places. Laura and I left Fiona at the Merrimac Ferry parking lot and she drove me twelve miles back into Lodi. The day's plan was to move north of the ferry, but I didn't want to be separated from Fiona by the river. What if the ferry shut down for some reason? It was already unusual for it to be running in December. What if today was the day ice began forming? If I wanted more miles later that afternoon, I'd bike.

I relished the glorious sunshine that brought freakishly warm weather. I clipped along the road that would lead to Gibraltar Rock, one of the most iconic segments of the trail. The segment with the tree. The famous, gnarled cedar tree sitting atop the butte overlooking the valley was one of the most photographed spots on the trail. I reached the southern trailhead of Gibraltar Rock and walked past the three cars in the lot. Oh well. I couldn't expect to have it all to myself on a Saturday.

I followed the trail to the top of the butte. A few hikers had come down the trail. We created a wide berth from each other while passing. Some wore masks. That's odd, I thought, remembering the mere three cars in the lot. The trail leveled off at the top of the butte where I abruptly stopped. The crowd was as dense as a 1980s Saturday at the mall. Oh my god, this is insane…all these people must have parked at the other end, I reasoned. Exploring the outdoors was the only thing to do anymore. Covid numbers surged through Wisconsin. I put on my mask for the first time while walking the trail.

At one of the most prized overlooks, a young couple had spread out a blanket, covering the whole rock. They drank coffee and played cards. Kids and families milled about, trying to get a glimpse of the panoramic view that the couple blocked. They sipped their coffee with an air of snootiness as if they knew they had something others wanted.

"Ya know there's kids waiting that would like pictures, right?" I said without thinking. It just blurted out. The last few years had tanked my tolerance level for people. The 2016 election. The response to Covid. Dealing with Mitch. I was over people. Sure, the couple had a right to be there. No sign said, don't take up the whole rock with a blanket and sit down for coffee. But what happened to being decent and letting kids take their fun selfies at the overlook? They rolled their eyes and didn't respond.

I took my turn to snap a quick photo of The Tree and then quickly moved through the crowd to find the trail. A steady stream of people hiked up as I headed down. I left my mask on as it was too steep in places to step aside. The trail ended at a packed parking lot. "Geez," I said. I was glad I did Devil's Lake during the week. Devil's Lake was just up the road and probably a madhouse. I walked past the cars in the lot and then stopped, totally gobsmacked at the site before me. Parked cars lined the side of the road like an endless snake. I walked past car after car, thankful that I wasn't locked into a Monday through Friday job where weekends had to be shared with the masses. I only had to tolerate a Saturday crowd once in a while.

Thanks to Laura's shuttle, I didn't lose time with a bike pick up after my hike. Fiona's tires rumbled onto the ferry and we left behind another county. As the ferry chugged across the river, I relaxed to the gentle rhythm and thought about my next move. I had only done twelve miles and hadn't used up energy biking. With a couple hours of daylight left, I certainly had the time to do more. But did I want to be searching for Mike and Sandy's place in the dark?

I chose to be done for the day and treat myself to a meal at the Broadway Diner in Baraboo. Being three in the afternoon, there were only two other people in the 1950s retro diner. I took a seat on a teal-blue stool, ordered a hamburger from the masked waitress and studied Google Maps for the land's location until my dinner basket arrived.

I drove out of town and found the Illinois couple's vacation house. Mike and Sandy had never met me, but yet they trusted me with their property. Their generosity acted as a healing salve. I forgave the coffee-sipping overlook-hoggers. I probably had been a coffee-sipping, overlook-hogger at times during my younger years as well.

I pulled into the driveway and poked around. My tent could go next to the house on the gravel driveway. A neighbor's home sat directly across the road. While I had permission to be there and could prove it with the texts on my phone, I didn't want to cause the neighbors concern. I found the dirt access road that would take me to their back woods and followed it until the deer stand came into view. I parked Fiona and walked through the tall, brown grass to check it out. The stand wasn't too high off the ground, maybe six feet. It would be cool to sleep in a deer stand as

SQUATTER

part of my trail experience. But it would be a lot of trouble getting my stuff up there.

I pitched my tent next to Fiona in the light of sunset. The warm December day slipped away and snippy, winter air took over. I changed into my leggings but left on my shirt layers as usual. My legs could tolerate the quick exposure to the cold air, but it was too much for my upper body. I rolled up my pants and set them at the foot of my sleeping bag. The night's low would be in the teens. I tucked my water bottle in between my two sleeping bags.

There was nothing to do but wait out the long, cold night. I pulled my bag over my head and my phone illuminated my dark cocoon. I opened my spam folder. Mitch didn't acknowledge my statement that his behavior felt like stalking. He just rambled on about how he'd changed.

I zipped my phone into my jacket pocket, balled the jacket up in between the sleeping bags and fell asleep to the yelping of coyotes. The winter wind pummeled my tent.

* * *

The following afternoon, I was about to start the third bike shuttle of the day that would begin the eastern bifurcation. In the middle of the state, the trail formed a loop, creating an east and west bifurcation. Only one side is required to become a Thousand Miler, the title granted to those who completed the trail. Like most things regarding my adventure, I didn't put much thought into the decision. I went with the shorter east side.

I pedaled onto Bluff Road without thinking about the name's implication. Bluff should have been a clue to check out the best biking direction. I'd rather walk up a hill than bike it. Sometimes blindly jumping in worked in my favor and sometimes it didn't. I pushed hard on the pedals as the road gradually inclined. Of course, Bluff Road was a hill. A long, never-ending hill. My muscles burned as I panted.

In between huffs and puffs I muttered, "This is bullshit."

I gave up, hopped off the bike, locked it to a tree and walked back down the hill to Fiona. I'd have to piecemeal the long inclining road together with multiple bike and hikes, making sure I was walking uphill rather than biking.

There really wasn't a great place to park where I had haphazardly left my bike. I loaded it up and drove on to find suitable parking on the shoulder. I spied a good spot just as I passed by it. The perfect place to end the day as Bluff Road would take a steep descent after that. I searched for a place to turn around.

I pulled into the short driveway of a country home. A man tinkered around near the garage and looked up at me in surprise. He stopped what he was doing and dashed to his truck as I backed out. I drove away and glanced in the rearview mirror. He was coming up behind me. Fast. Eh… coincidence, I thought. Maybe he suddenly remembered he needed something at Fleet Farm. I pulled over in the spot I had passed and made sure Fiona was completely off the road. The man in the truck pulled up behind me.

In my side mirror, I watched the guy step out of his truck and march toward me. He looked like he meant business. I glanced at his hands to see if he carried a weapon. He didn't. You never know what people are thinking. Maybe I drove the same truck as his no-good brother-in-law who owed him money. Or his daughter's ex-boyfriend who had done her wrong. Or maybe I was the tenth person to turn around in his driveway that day and he was gonna lose his shit.

He didn't have a weapon, and I wanted to park there, so I felt it best to roll down the window and see what was up.

SQUATTER

"WHADAYA DOIN'?!" he bellowed as he walked up the side of Fiona. When our eyes met, his strained expression gave way to surprise. His body language instantly relaxed. "Oh gosh, you're a woman," he stammered.

"Yeah. I'm hiking the Ice Age Trail," I said, reaching for the handy-dandy guidebook. "And road walks need to be done." The guy was a homeowner along the road that I needed to walk and park on today and the next day so I thought it was best to be polite. He glanced at my bike in Fiona's bed. "I use my bike to shuttle myself," I said, reading his mind.

"You know, there are a good amount of walkers on this road," he said, contemplating my explanation. "I'm sorry ma'am. I chased after you because we've had a problem with poachers and trespassers in the area. So, all the neighbors have been on the lookout. I saw your blaze-orange through the windshield when you were turning around and needed to check it out."

"I completely understand," I replied. "I'll be parked here in the morning as well, heading in the other direction."

When he walked away, I ripped a piece of paper out of my notebook and wrote, *Hiking Ice Age Trail, for parking issues call....* I added my number and tossed it on the dash with my guidebook. That would be my plan going forward when doing road walks where I wasn't parked at a trailhead.

The two hours for me to bike and hike four miles of Bluff Road put me in the mood for a take-out dinner. The never-ending hill and the landowner thinking I was a poacher stressed me out and I wanted comfort food. I picked up grilled cheese and fries and drove to Mike and Sandy's land in the dark. Lights from a distant house twinkled in the night. I turned off my headlights. Last night I arrived before dark so I didn't worry about neighbors seeing my lights at the edge of the woods. I didn't need any more confrontations.

I ate my grilled cheese in the driver's seat and then stepped out into the biting December wind. Orion, the hunter constellation, had taken his dominant place in the winter night sky. I began setting up my tent. My fingers grew numb as I clipped the tent to the poles, fumbling a bit as the wind kept taking hold of the tent. The frozen ground resisted as I pushed in the stakes. I stood alongside Fiona to change into my leggings. I tried to shield myself from the wind, but the icy air stung my bare legs. For some reason that I don't remember, I didn't change in the shelter of the tent. Maybe I thought it was faster to jump into them right then and there. I hated the idea of sleeping in my hiking pants because honestly, after peeing in the woods I imagined some of it had to splatter. I brushed my teeth, filled my water bottle and crawled into my double sleeping bags to wait out the long, cold night. I had a strange need to be uncomfortable. I believed the discomfort would force me to grow. If I wasn't challenged, then doing the trail was just a vacation and nothing internal would be accomplished.

* * *

Cold morning bike shuttles pretty much suck. I parked where the upset homeowner followed me to the night before, covered my face with my gaiter and pedaled off toward the Lower Narrows of Sauk County. The icy air cut through my boots as I pedaled, freezing my toes. Steel-gray skies had stolen the unusual, glorious stretch of weather we had been gifted. I turned onto a busy state highway. I was actually thankful for its uphill grade. Walking my bike for a bit warmed my feet.

SQUATTER

I approached the large gap in the land called the Lower Narrows. A major gorge created by water millions of years ago. I turned onto a quiet county highway and rounded a curve that entered a vast valley. Dark clouds containing snow squalls hung low over the land. I heard an unfamiliar, steady, low sound coming from the valley. Up ahead, the valley floor was moving.

I pedaled closer. Curiosity made me forget my cold feet. The sound grew to a thunderous volume that made me feel small. Snow pelted my face as I pedaled through a squall. I stopped to gaze at the scene before me. Tens of thousands, maybe a million sandhill cranes spanned the entire valley. I stopped on the road, completely surrounded by the fascinating creatures. Their collective voices rang through the valley so loudly that if I were to yell, my voice would have been soaked up and never heard. Small flocks randomly rose up out of the mass and flew in unison a short distance before landing. I stood in awe with a surreal feeling of being a speck among the sea of birds who graciously tolerated my presence. I got back on my bike and crept along, taking in the wonder of it all. The cranes closest to the road did not seem threatened by my presence. Why should they? There were millions of them and one of me.

I pedaled across the valley and up the other side, continuing my planned miles. After locking my bike to a road sign near a bright red barn, I began the return walk, eager to see the cranes again. A family of goats curiously watched me pass; their heads comically moved in unison. About a mile from the valley, I heard the collective bugling of the cranes. I emerged from the wooded hills. White patches of snow squalls hung over the valley. I left the warmer, wooded bluff and descended into the valley's cold air. I pulled my gaiter over my face as a snow squall engulfed me. The cranes stood stoically in the swirling snow.

    I could check off another county as complete. I had been out for four nights, and Fiona smelled like dirty socks. When I pulled into the driveway, the traffic signs that Mitch left were laying on top of the retaining wall.

18

*The trail is mentally making me stronger,
but it's physically wearing me down.*

The middle of the state contained long road walks. A lot of them. Most weren't far from the interstate, making them easy day trips from home. I broke up the bike shuttles throughout the day to keep my feet from becoming ice blocks. The winter air cut through my boots as I pedaled. I couldn't take more than five miles of biking at a time. Bike, walk back. Bike some more. Walk back. Repeat, until I completed about fifteen miles or so.

In the Facebook group, people mentioned hand and feet warmers. If I would have taken two minutes to find out what warmers were and driven the five minutes to Fleet Farm to buy them, I could have maybe slipped them into my boots and avoided the whole freezing feet issue. But I couldn't get my mind to focus on figuring out those things.

Mitch's emails had ramped up. The more I stayed silent, the more he sent. Apologies, promises of change, professions of love, and clips of him singing. He said he had a dream that I was with someone else and asked if it was true. *I sincerely hope that you never betrayed our intimacy,* he wrote. When I didn't answer he pressed. *Did my dream depict reality?* I hated being accused of things I didn't do. So, I sent a simple answer. *I never betrayed us.*

I passed seven hundred miles on December 13. At least a dozen Amish buggies rode past me on that Sunday afternoon as I walked the roads. The clippity clop of horses' hooves echoed far down the road. Each family waved and curious young faces peeked out from the black buggies as they passed me. That would be the last day in December that I would hike. The many miles of recent pavement pounding had caused persistent pain on the top of my left foot. I iced it in the evenings, but it always returned. I ran my fingers over the top of my foot. No sudden sharp pain. That was good. Then it wasn't a stress fracture. But I did read about stress injury, the precursor to stress fracture. The long road walk miles had taken its toll. I rolled my eyes, pissed at myself. There were athletes out there who pushed their bodies to the limit and here I was, just walking, and something was wrong.

* * *

I gifted myself a ring for Christmas. A gold band embedded with tiny diamonds. Seven hundred miles and no more seeing Mitch. I was worthy of better, so I called the ring my Worthiness Ring. Mitch sent me a Christmas card and on Christmas Day, sent an email at 11:11 that simply said, *I love you.* He often sent emails at 11:11 saying that it was his special time. I answered, *Your behavior is becoming creepy. You've become a stalker. Knock it off.*

On January 3, I decided to give my foot a trial run. I spent the day in a black-and-white world on the roads of the Eastern Bifurcation. Rime ice coated the trees, fencing, and signs. Snow blanketed the fields. The sky remained a deep steel gray for the whole day, making me wonder if the sun ever rose at all. The yellow dividing line in the road was the only color. Like an edited black-and-white photo with one area colored in. My foot started bothering me on the drive home. I iced it that evening and planned to go out for multiple days starting on January 5.

My plan to finish the trail was to return to the bottom of the state and make a beeline up to the Eastern Terminus in Door County, Wisconsin's "thumb." I would finish up the mid-state's bifurcation somewhere in there.

On a foggy January morning, I met the chapter coordinator at the Arbor Ridge Trailhead for a shuttle ride to complete a long road walk that would bring me to the outskirts of Janesville. Wisconsin's Covid rates were high. I sat in the backseat as we drove through the thick fog while wearing masks with the windows cracked. Every shuttle driver had their preference and I gladly obliged. I would've strapped myself to the roof in order to get a shuttle ride on a winter day.

"The rime ice is gorgeous," I commented and told him about the rime ice I experienced a few days ago.

"We've had an unusual amount of that this winter," he said. "Many mistake it for hoarfrost, but rime ice is common with fog." He talked more about the difference and how fog's droplets freeze and cling to everything. "Hoarfrost is similar to dew and happens on clear nights." My shuttle rides were often mini classroom sessions with people that not only loved the trail, but knew a lot about nature. I appreciated the few minutes to learn something new.

"This is the spot," I said when we came to where I had left off back in November.

"Ok, see you for tomorrow's ride," he said, and dropped me off on the snow-covered road. His car was soon swallowed up by the mist. Thick, creamy soup engulfed everything. The road disappeared into the unknown a few feet from me. The fog not only hid the world, it also absorbed its sound.

The extreme silence felt strange, almost a bit disturbing. I'd experienced the lack of sound in narrow canyons out west. Almost like the soundproof rooms technicians use for hearing tests. We're surrounded by subtle noises all the time, even in quiet settings and don't realize it until it's gone.

I stood in the silent, gray world coated in magical ice as if I'd been plopped onto a deserted planet. I imagined my winter gear was the attire of a fighting warrior on a quest to save something important: the Old World, an oracle or a magical gemstone. Monsters and aliens hid on this foggy planet, waiting for battle and guarding the secret that would save the universe. I took my first steps toward saving the world and realized the lightly traveled country road was icy. My superhero fantasy ended, and I returned to being a fifty-two-year-old grandma, with a sore foot, carefully navigating the ice to avoid breaking anything.

The fog gave up its hidden treasures as I walked. Barns, farm houses, a lone horse, cows gathered by a fence would emerge from the mist, only to vanish again after I passed. Like a carousel of images that were available for a momentary view and then would disappear. By mid-morning, my stomach growled for the cashew butter sandwich in my pack. I ate it standing at the side of the road.

By noon, I needed to find a place to sit for a few minutes. I spotted a gray cable box along a fence. Getting to it would mean trudging through knee-deep snow, but I needed to sit on that box. I sunk into the snow past my knees and sat with relief. I studied the rime ice that adorned the barbed-wire fencing. The delicate crystals created stunning artwork. Billions of crystals coated everything in my world on an average Wednesday in January.

SQUATTER

I reached Fiona after five-and-a-half hours of road walking. My foot felt okay. I boiled water on the tailgate and then sat in the driver's seat eating an oatmeal lunch. My phone pinged. A text from my oldest son, Jory.

Are you home? Turn on the TV.

I'm eating at a trailhead outside of Janesville. What's going on? I wrote.

It was January 6, 2021, and he explained the turmoil happening at the Capitol Building in Washington, D.C. I tried to access various news sites, but they wouldn't load. I was just outside of Janesville. Not in the middle of nowhere. Jory continued to fill me in while I decided on my afternoon plan.

The Devil's Staircase segment created somewhat of a loop and followed along the Rock River. I could jump ahead to hike it that afternoon and easily bypass it the next day.

Virginia is sending in troops.

At Riverside Park where I'd pick up Devil's Staircase, cell service improved. I watched the news footage of what was unfolding in DC. How much more turmoil and disruption could we take? I told my son I had more miles to go and to keep me updated.

As the segment's name suggested, Devil's Staircase had a long, steep staircase. Winter was in full swing, and that meant treacherous trail stairs. I pulled on my Fleet Farm spikes over my boots. They would have been helpful that morning on the slick road, but I had left them with Fiona. My spikes weren't expensive doodads. They had been one of those go-with-what-you-know purchases. Years ago, John had a weekly paper route and we bought those cheap spikes for him because it was all we could afford. They kept him from biffing out on icy sidewalks, so I bought myself a pair and they worked well.

What wasn't working well was that both pairs of my hiking boots got damp and heavy in the snow. They were water resistant, but not waterproof. I even treated them with water repellent spray. Tired of slogging through snow with heavy feet, I made a mental note to order waterproof winter hiking boots when I got home.

A sheet of ice coated the staircase. Snow had built up on the steps, forming a hard-packed, gigantic slide. I carefully climbed, pulling myself up with the railing. The trail cut along a steep hillside overlooking the Rock River. A wrong step would mean a long tumble to the river. My phone continued to buzz in my pocket with DC updates from my son.

People shot. Maryland deploying troops. Talk of the 25th amendment.

I took another Aleve and started the hour drive north to Laura's garage while my boots dried beneath the floorboard heat. Soon, I'd have to figure out another place to stay. Curling my left leg up on the seat with a cold pack on my foot, I drove and listened to NPR recap the day's events from Washington, D.C.

* * *

When I awoke the next morning, my face felt raw and tight. Windburn. The prior day wasn't particularly windy, but those long, cold hours in a light breeze was enough to make my skin raw. I slathered Vaseline on my face after getting dressed and drove the hour back down to the trailhead. The morning was a repeat of the day before. Rime ice, fog, and a shuttle ride. I got dropped off seventeen miles away. The Janesville segment would be ten miles for the day. I expected it to be an easy city walk.

Heavy snow had come through before my arrival and much of the Janesville segment hadn't been cleared or even walked by anyone. After all, who would want to go for a winter walk in fields behind giant box stores? I had imagined the trail would be along sidewalks. But of course, if I had consulted the guidebook…

I broke miles of trail through knee-deep snow. Even though it was twenty degrees, sweat poured down my back and chest, as I panted from the exertion. I whipped off my puffy coat and stuffed it in my pack while taking a moment to catch my breath. My boots grew heavier as they soaked up the snow. The trail eventually led through neighborhoods free of deep snow.

I recalled that there might be an old well on the Janesville segment. I say might because I vaguely remembered someone mentioning it on Facebook. I knew nothing about what it looked like or where it was. Passing through downtown, I spied a simple red, metal spigot sticking out from the side of a snow mound. Maybe that was it. It was an ordinary, common spigot, but there could've been a plaque hidden underneath the snow saying: This is the site of the first well in Janesville dug by Old Farmer Hanson… or something like that. I took a picture of it because I didn't want to miss having documented passing the historic well site.

At Riverside Park, where the segment ended, I spied a low, wide stone structure in the snow. I noticed it the day before, but it didn't pique my interest enough to want to plod through the snow. I didn't have the energy to check out every random thing that caught my attention. But now the well was on my mind and my boots were already wet. I high stepped it through the snow. The stone structure turned out to be a beautiful oasis of water in the January snow. Water flowed from a pipe, filling the large, stone pool. I laughed and shook my head at the idea that the red spigot could have been "the well" others mentioned.

While eating a dried dinner in the driver's seat, with a cold pack on my throbbing foot, I mulled over the night's plans. I zoomed in on Google Maps, searching for camping. Either stealth or a campground that might be plowed. Nothing. I didn't want to drive the hour to Laura's and then back again in the morning. Getting a room for the first time on the trail might have to be the night's option. Janesville had a Motel 6. The chain had been removing their carpeting and making improvements. Sketchy motel carpeting was something I couldn't do. Weird odors made me reach for my inhaler. I dialed their number.

"Janesville Motel 6," a cheery voice answered.

"Do your rooms have carpet?" I asked.

"No ma'am, all of our rooms are bare floor," she said.

"Great, I'll take a room for tonight," I said, and headed their way.

The lady behind the heavy plexiglass divider assigned me a room. Rolling through the lot, Fiona and I passed rusty, dented, well-used cars. Most were not from the current decade. Heck, maybe not even from the current century. Fiona definitely would be the nicest vehicle in the lot. I didn't want her to be the target for a break-in. We rolled past room after room until I saw my number. In the very back of the motel. Next to the dumpsters. Two men in hoodies stood nearby. Small groups of three or four, men and women, huddled together in the cold, smoking outside various rooms.

Not wanting to draw attention to myself as a solo female, I pulled up my own hoodie and tucked my braids inside. After grabbing my overnight stuff, I walked straight into the room, locking the door behind me. I paused, thinking for a moment. Fiona stood out from the rest of the vehicles, and my bike was in the bed. I didn't like being back there. I drove back to the office and asked if they had any rooms closer to the front. The lady behind the thick glass gave an understanding nod. "Here ya go," she said, sliding me a new key card under the glass window.

I backed Fiona up as close as I could to room 109 and hoped my bike would still be there in the morning. People huddled together in the walkway with lit cigarettes and welcomed others as they joined them. A man walked past me, giving a casual, how-ya-doin' nod with a "Hey." I gave my own confident nod and replied, "Hey."

Sitting on the edge of the bed, the sound of a crying baby and children's chatter filtered through the thin walls. That's when it dawned on me that families lived there. In the Motel 6. That explained why those, huddling outside for a smoke, knew each other. We often got patients at the hospital who lived in motels. My heart felt heavy at the thought that there were families who had to call a Motel 6 home.

I placed my wet boots by the heater, slipped out of my Crocs and put my sock feet up on the bed while I Googled a place that would deliver food. The lasagna I had a few hours ago wasn't holding me. My feet didn't feel right. Not just the top of my left foot, but both feet felt odd. I kept them up on the pillow. I dialed a place. "Yeah, I'll have a turkey sub, chips, and a root beer," I said. "An hour's fine." I'm not a regular soda drinker, but a root beer sounded delicious.

The weird feeling in my feet persisted as I stood in the shower. I reached for my glasses on the vanity and looked down. My feet were swollen. I'd just spent the last couple of weeks resting. The pavement was killing me.

* * *

I opened the motel door to the morning darkness. The ol' Schwinn still lay in Fiona's bed. Even though I had shuttle rides planned for every morning of that trip out, I still brought the bike just in case.

The swelling in my feet had resolved during the night. I slathered my raw face in Vaseline and ate breakfast at the trailhead. No rime ice that morning, but heavy gloom. I hadn't seen even a sliver of the sun in the last few days. It would be another seventeen-mile day, most of it pavement for a road walk and the town of Milton.

After shuffling through the snow of the wooded Clover Valley segment, my boots grew heavy as the snow clinging to them melted. Then, the dreary, ten-mile road walk began. The relentless wind swept across the open fields and stung my already raw face. I pulled my gaiter up over my nose and tucked it under my glasses, making sure it protected my cheeks. The fabric felt gross against my sticky Vaseline skin. I kept my head down and willed my feet to keep moving. The miserable cold and wind sapped my desire to search for a podcast. I listened to the howling wind.

In Milton, I came to a three-story, white building with green trim. The Milton House, a National Historic Landmark built in 1844, was Wisconsin's only documented stop on the Underground Railroad. I doubted it would be open, but I walked up to the door anyway. Locked. The sign on the door said to ring the bell for assistance. I put on my mask and pushed the button.

"Hello," a lady greeted me as she cracked open the door to the gusts. Her smile could be heard from behind her mask. She hugged herself as the wind lashed at her.

"Is the museum open?" I asked.

SQUATTER

She confirmed what I suspected. She glanced down at my hiking poles and boots.

"I'm hiking the Ice Age Trail and just thought I'd stop to get out of the wind," I said.

"You're welcome to come in and browse the exhibits in the front hall," she said with a touch of sympathy in her voice. I thanked her and stepped inside. The door closed, shutting out the wind's roar.

My footsteps echoed through the strikingly silent museum hall. After hours of listening to the steady drone of wind, I welcomed the quiet and wandered the exhibits. Worn, colorless photos, capturing people during a fleeting moment of their hard-working lives, hung on the walls. Relics from the past lay neatly arranged in glass cases. A farmer paused from his never-ending work to pose for the rare opportunity of having a photograph taken. What would he have thought if he knew his image would be viewed by future strangers? A delicate, porcelain doll sat behind glass. Maybe it was a Christmas gift for a little girl who had been eyeing it in the general store. Would she have believed her doll would someday sit in a glass case for upcoming generations to enjoy? I pondered all that and willed myself through time to connect with those whose lives were represented in the museum hall.

* * *

My feet felt weird again as Fiona came into view. I collapsed into the front seat. My feet were swollen again. This foot business wasn't good. The best decision was to go home a day early. Dammit.

19

The desert is calling.

A year had passed since I flew into Las Vegas for my Death Valley trip. With my foot bothering me, I needed a break from the trail's long road miles. But I needed to do something. As much as I knew Mitch was bad for me, the comfort of familiarity had always drawn me back.

Leisurely desert hiking sounded good for a trail break. Liz and Grace were welcome to join me. But they weren't into outdoorsy adventures. I had traveled a lot with them: New York City, Washington DC, Los Angeles. Those were the types of trips they liked. But city trips during Covid weren't gonna happen. So, I planned a solo trip of two nights camping then two nights in a small yurt on a ranch. I purchased a round trip ticket to Las Vegas for $95. With empty seats on both sides of me and my face covered with a mask, I landed in Vegas. At the rental car place, the clerk handed me a key fob and told me where to find my Ford Explorer.

Sitting in the front seat, I studied the dash of my temporary ride. How do you turn it on, I wondered. I saw a button labeled Start and pushed it. Nothing. Fiona was newer, but basic, so she came with a key. I'd never driven a keyless vehicle before. My sons could tell me how to start it, but being on the lower level of the parking garage, the calls wouldn't go through. I glanced through the windshield at the sea of cars. No human being in sight. "Are you kidding me?" I murmured. "Am I really gonna have to go find an employee and ask them how to start this car?"

I wandered the parking garage until someone wearing a rental car vest came into view. "Excuse me! Ummm, I rented a car, but…ahh, I don't know how to start it," I said while laughing at my own ineptness.

"Oh no worries!" said the smiling young lady. "We get that all the time. Especially from older people."

Nice.

After learning that the brake pedal needed to be depressed while pressing the start button, I drove to Valley of Fire State Park, forty-five minutes northeast of Las Vegas. With it being a weekday in January, I didn't make a camping reservation. The next day I planned to meet up with a hiker named Alan from a worldwide Facebook hiking group. The meeting wasn't a "date" and we both knew it. I wanted to meet new people who loved hiking. He had hiked and camped with others from the group and they lived to tell the tale.

I drove through the stunning red desert of the park and wound my way through the various campgrounds. Every site at every campground was taken. The afternoon shadows grew long when I walked into the ranger station to ask for suggestions on where to stay.

"With Covid, it's been non-stop crazy," said the ranger, "you could try the mesa on the BLM land a few miles outside of the park."

"BLM?" I asked.

"Bureau of Land Management," she replied. I knew about free, dispersed camping at national forests and grasslands, but BLM land was new to me. Apparently, it's all over the West.

"Is it safe?" I asked.

"Oh yeah," she said, "Just drive and you'll see other people out on the mesa."

So, I drove. And like she said, in the distance sat two camping trailers out in the desert. I turned onto Sand Mine Road with a sign that read 4x4 recommended and picked a random spot on the vast mesa to set up my tent. The dry, cracked earth would not accept my tent stakes, so I piled rocks around them. Hopefully that would do the trick. A deep gorge cut through the earth, yards from where I parked. The sunset's glow enhanced the gorge's rich, red, rocky sides.

I took photos of my camp. Photos of my dinner. Photos of the glorious desert sunset. I was rocking the solo camping thing out in the Nevada desert. I pranced around chanting, "I'm awesome, I'm awesome."

Until the sun went down and the wind kicked up.

While in my sleeping bag, I listened to the wind roar across the mesa. It scooped up sand and pelted it against my tent. The wind blasts forced the sand underneath the rainfly and through the tent's netting, coating my face with grit. I covered my head with my bag and prepared for a long night. The wind blew the tent nearly flat over me. The gusts came in rhythmic cycles. Almost like ocean waves, where the waves cyclically build and decline. In the cocoon of my sleeping bag, my cell phone glowed. Only nine o'clock.

"I can't do this all night," I mumbled. I sat up and braced my hand on the tent wall that blew inward. Sand coated my sleeping bag and the tent floor.

I stepped out into the sandstorm. Needles of grit blasted my exposed skin. Across the mesa, the cozy lights of the two campers twinkled through the sand clouds. Smart people who would never set up a tent on top of a desert mesa.

SQUATTER

In between the wave-like gusts, I scooped up my sleeping gear and threw it into the Explorer. I snatched up the tent stakes from underneath the ridiculously placed stones, while keeping hold of the tent with one hand. My teeth became gritty and sand pelted my glasses. Facing the wind so the tent would blow against my body and not disappear into the gorge, I wrestled the tent into a ball and tossed it into the backseat. I plopped into the driver's seat, stunned. Grit crackled inside of my mouth. Dust fell out of my hair. I just sat there. Panting. What now? It was almost nine-thirty. Why didn't I just get an Airbnb? What was I thinking? I could drive into a town and get a hotel. No. Don't give up. I turned to glance at the dusty mess in the back of the Explorer. "Maybe I can sleep in here."

I climbed into the back and carefully folded up the tent. Puffs of dust rose from the fabric with each fold. With the backseats down and my camping mattress rolled out, I sat back to assess.

"It's gonna work!"

I looked at the gap between the seats. If my head was to the back, the mattress would support my legs over the gap. I stretched out on my new bed. "This is fantastic! Why didn't I think of this first?" Snuggling up in my mini fortress, I fell asleep while the sand and wind pummeled the Explorer. The rear license plate rattled loose and flapped in the wind throughout the night, permeating my dreams.

* * *

I met Alan at the entrance to Valley of Fire before sunrise.

"Yooooolandaaa!" he said as he got out of his car. A little beater type car. He looked just like he did in his adventure photos. A tall, lean guy, beaming a smile through a weather worn face with tufts of sun-kissed hair sticking out from a beanie.

"Alannnn!" I replied, and we gave each other a quick, turn-your-head-away Covid hug. Online friendships sometimes get a bad rap. But Alan was like a comfy sweatshirt where I could be real.

Alan showed me a little-known-pink-colored slot canyon hidden in the park. We leisurely hiked some of the more popular trails before the crowds arrived. No big miles or pounding the pavement. My feet were doing fine. We left the park and I followed him down long, dusty roads to BLM land near Lake Mead for the night. He built a fire and we sat under the desert stars.

"Yolanda, I think you were the only person on that plane not looking for money, sex, or drugs," Alan laughed.

"Yep, just a hiker geek coming to Vegas," I said.

"I think you women can sometimes be just as bad as the guys," Alan said. "In my experience, it's the women who initiate sex most of the time." He told hilarious tales about his middle-aged dating woes. We roared with laughter until the fire faded.

"Do you know how freaking fun it is to just chill like this?" he asked. I nodded. He was right. It was freaking fun.

No awkwardness or tension hung in the air. No expectations for something more. No wondering if the other person was going to make a move. Never once do I remember being in one-on-one male company that centered on friendship. I drank in his stories. My late teen years were a mess, then I had spent my entire life unhappily married. And then there was Mitch. I needed to experience that being in male company could be fun. Fun and nothing else. The temperature plunged after the sun went down. I crawled into my makeshift bed in the Explorer and Alan went to his tent. We were in a bit of a narrow valley. He must have known you don't pitch a tent on a mesa.

SQUATTER

* * *

I said goodbye to Alan the next day after a long hike through a canyon near Lake Mead. Cleopatra's Wash, he called it. I followed him back to the edge of Las Vegas and we pulled into a gas station. We hugged, and I thanked him for showing me his favorite camping area. I appreciated him more than he could know.

I drove to Sandy Valley Ranch just over the border in California in the Mojave Desert. Mountains silhouetted the horizon. I passed under the gate bearing the ranch's name and found the little glamping yurt I reserved set amongst the brush and sand. As with every place else, Covid hit all businesses hard. Visitors were down at the ranch, which is why the glamping yurt was reduced to $25 a night. But the daily operation of a working ranch carried on. I passed Spanish speaking ranch workers on my way to the empty dining room where I ate alone.

January nights in the desert often got down into the twenties. I walked under desert stars to the outdoor sink near the back of the property and reached underneath for water to brush my teeth. "We had some pipes break after freezing a couple weeks ago," Dana, a ranch worker, had told me when she greeted me on my arrival. She showed me how to get the water from under the sink, behind the break. The inconvenience didn't phase me. I was the queen of making-do. I returned to the cozy yurt, turned on the space heater provided and snuggled into the little bed.

The following two days, I explored desert towns, cemeteries, petroglyphs, and did some light hiking. My foot got the rest it needed, and I had kept myself occupied. As I packed up the Explorer, Dana approached me from her camper not far from the yurt.

"Did you have a good visit?" she asked, clutching her robe closed to keep out the morning air. A bandana covered her head, protecting it from desert dust.

"I did. The ranch is lovely," I said, pausing from my packing.

"I have a gift for you," she said, and handed me a horseshoe with an orange ribbon tied around it. SVR (Sandy Valley Ranch) 2021 was written in permanent marker on the metal. "This horseshoe has been all over all these mountains and holds its good energy," she glanced at the distant mountains silhouetted in the morning sun. "I get a sense that you could use its magic."

* * *

I once again sat on a near-empty plane as it took off from Las Vegas. My backpack held the horseshoe from Dana that radiated good mountain energy and my heart held the lighthearted friendship offered from Alan. Both aided me in my healing journey.

20

I had the most difficult day yet on the trail, making me wonder what the hell I'm doing out here.

My feet had time to recover and I returned to the trail in late January. Mitch's emails kept coming. A permanent fixture in my life. One was exceptionally drawn out, detailing his life's woes. I skimmed over the words. Always the same stuff.

* * *

I needed to start planning where to spend the trail nights. Winging it wasn't going to work, especially with winter camping options difficult to find. Financially, regular motels weren't an option. I posted in the Facebook group asking for garages or yards to sleep in. And to my surprise, people offered. I would have a new garage to sleep in for the next two nights.

My winter hiking boots came while I was in Nevada. My first day back would be an easy bike and hike on a five-mile road walk along with some trail miles. I pulled into the trailhead parking lot on a thirteen-degree morning. Fiona's tires crunched along the hard-packed snow. The milky-white sky was barely distinguishable from the snowy horizon. I slathered my face with Vaseline and started my bike shuttle.

Fifteen minutes into the ride, I had only gone a mile and a half. Icy patches on the snow-packed road and wicked wind kept my speed at a crawl. Up ahead, the road disappeared. I pedaled closer. Maybe my eyes were playing tricks on me in the world of white.

The road ended at a field laced with snow drifts. It just disappeared. What the heck? I thought. This was the suggested connecting route. Guthook confirmed that I was on Island Drive and that it would connect with Anderson Road. Maybe Island Drive was a dirt road that wasn't plowed in winter. I stared at the frozen tundra. My jaw tightened. The wind bit my face and blew walls of snow across the field that resembled an Arctic wasteland. Cold seeped through my layers of clothing since I wasn't generating heat.

There was no way I could slog my bike through that field. With my back to the wind, I pulled off my mittens, hunched over my phone and searched for a different route. "If I take Highway 89 south, then cut over, I could take Kettle Moraine Drive to the turnoff for the segment," I mumbled. Maybe it was the cold and blowing snow. Maybe it was the brain fog I suffered. Either way, it didn't occur to me that biking a road named Kettle Moraine Drive wouldn't be a good idea, since kettles and moraines meant hills. I also missed the fact that going north for a tiny bit on Highway 89 would have gotten me to Anderson Road and back on track for the suggested road route. I just couldn't think straight.

The cold seeped through my new boots as I pedaled. They may have been waterproof, but they weren't icy-air proof. My feet graduated from cold to painful. I pushed my bike up the relentless hills, partially because the Schwinn was so darn heavy, but walking allowed my feet to get a break from the wind. Cottages dotted the rolling landscape, overlooking frozen lakes. I hoped for a store or gas station where I could take a break from the cold. My feet were painful blobs. I pedaled harder. My lungs heaved in the frigid air. While coasting down a hill, I sang goofy songs to keep my mind off the pain.

"I come from Alabama with my banjo on my knee…"

Was that a business up ahead?

"I'm going to Louisiana, my true love for to see…"

Yes, it was!

"Please be open, please be open," I chanted, while flying down the hill and into the parking lot of JNT's Marine Pros. A boat store. The open sign in the window made me giddy. I rolled up to the door, clunked down the kickstand and hobbled inside wearing my oversized, blaze-orange shirt over my winter gear. I had pulled my pack straps so tight that it created odd puffs where a body shouldn't have puffs. A lady approached me and I tipped my head in all directions trying to see her through my foggy lenses. I certainly didn't look like someone about to buy a boat.

"Can I help you?" she asked in a friendly tone. Thank goodness.

"I'm biking to one of the Ice Age trailheads and wondered if I could just stand here a bit to warm up?" I said, still tilting my head, trying to see her.

She nodded and smiled. Sunshine poured in through the glass door, and I stood with my feet inside the sunny square. I really wanted to collapse onto the floor, rip off my boots and cradle my frozen toes in my hands. But that would be bad for their business. So, I swayed back and forth while standing in the sunny spot, my feet tingling as they warmed. After twenty minutes, I had thawed enough to continue.

My anticipated thirty-minute bike shuttle had turned into a two-hour ordeal. I arrived at the trailhead, elated that the bike ride was over. Thank goodness the next two days would be car shuttles. Heavy snow had recently fallen. Someone had broken in the trail before me, but it wasn't packed down from high usage. I plodded through the snow, trying to stay in the previous person's tracks, for an hour and a half. My new boots stayed dry.

I welcomed the following flat and easy road walk, that I would have biked if Island Drive hadn't vanished into a snowy abyss. I was eager to learn the mystery of the disappearing road. Turning onto a new road, I noticed two cars pull into a lot up ahead. People stood filling jugs with water flowing from a pipe stuck into a pile of rocks. The water flowed down onto metal grates before gliding its way through the woods to join Whitewater Creek. Another artesian well. Apparently, there were a number of them in the southern part of the state. The sign in the parking lot read:

Flowing Well

In 1895 the well was hand dug by Adam Channing. The original depth was 55'. It has been flowing steadily to this day.

I decided I would drive back to eat dinner at the well and exchange my tap-water-filled jugs from home for the well water. I pulled my gaiter up over my face and continued on. The roaring wind sweeping across sleeping fields would be a force I would reckon with on road walks for the entire winter. A herd of cows gathered at the fence line as I approached. I sang to them. "Oh Suzanna, oh don't you cry for me…" Their heads moved in unison as I walked past. My new fan club.

SQUATTER

I came to a fence post with the trail's yellow arrow nailed to it. The yellow arrow pointed to a field. No road. Maybe it was farther up. Nothing. I checked Guthook. The GPS arrow indicated that I stood at the right spot. Some of the snow drifts looked mighty deep. The alternative was to continue on to Highway 89–the short reroute that I should have biked earlier. But 89 would be busy with after-work and school traffic. I chose to trudge through the field.

All the energy I expended for the day only gained me 7.6 trail miles, but I did pass the 800-mile mark. I drove back to the Flowing Well, rehydrated a dried-beef stroganoff dinner and watched a steady stream of people fill their water jugs. After eating, I emptied my water bladder and got in line for a share of the liquid magic. The couple in front of me waited on multiple five-gallon jugs to fill. The woman glanced at my water bladder.

"You doin' the trail?" She asked.

"Yeah, I passed here earlier and decided to stop back. Lots of people come for this water," I said in surprise.

"Some come an hour or more every couple of weeks. Even from Illinois. My great-grandmother knew Adam Channing, the digger of the well," she said. "Our family's been here for generations." We chatted some more until their jugs filled. They drove away with a wave and I filled up my water jugs, thinking about what she said. Our family's been here for generations. I come from a disjointed, unconnected family and wondered what connection to family and a place felt like.

I typed in the Elkhorn address for my new garage accommodations and left the well. Robyn had said yes to a stranger on Facebook asking to sleep in a garage. She was a Thousand Miler, having finished the trail a few months before

I started. I pulled into Robyn's garage and we greeted each other while wearing masks.

"Hi Yolanda!" She said, as if we were old friends meeting again.

I handed her a jar of Wausau maple syrup and stepped back, not wanting her to regret saying yes during Covid. After showing me the logistics of the lights, the garage door opener and access to a basement bathroom, she left me for the night. The night's low was forecasted to be near zero. I read that the temperature in an unheated, attached garage was about ten degrees warmer than outside.

In the morning, I peeked out from my bag and zinged fully awake after breathing in the shockingly cold air. "Holy night!" I said in disbelief. I slipped on my Crocs and hopped over to Fiona in my long underwear, grabbed my pants and jumped back into the bag, stuffing them in with me to warm up. Moments later, I pulled on my lukewarm pants, tossed my sleeping gear into the backseat, folded up the cot and fired up Fiona as the garage doors lifted, letting in a blast of winter.

In a convenience store parking lot, I braided my hair, brushed my teeth and rinsed my face before driving to the trailhead for breakfast. I didn't want to disturb Robyn's family early in the morning. Matt from the Facebook group would be shuttling me. My phone buzzed in my pocket.

I'm here, Matt texted.

I'm here, too, I responded and glanced around thinking he might have pulled up alongside me.

Where are you? He wrote.

In the parking lot. Where are you?

In the parking lot.

SQUATTER

Apparently, there were two parking lots on that road. We corrected our mistake and I left Fiona behind to wait for me. Matt dropped me off for a nearly sixteen-mile day to hike the segments of Blue Spring Lake, Blackhawk, and the remainder of Whitewater Lake. No road walking.

"Text me when you finish so I know you're safe," Matt said with a wave.

"Will do. Thanks for the ride," I said, and closed the door.

My toes were numb with cold for the first hour. I marched through the snow to generate heat, keeping step with the one set of footprints in the deep snow. I hadn't expected so much up and down. If I had read the guidebook, I probably wouldn't have chosen to do sixteen snowy miles through the hilly Kettle Moraine area.

Midway through the segment, the tracks ended. Whoever hiked before me had turned back. I would have to break trail with snow nearly reaching my knees. I owned snowshoes. But for reasons I don't recall, I didn't have them with me. The trudging consumed all my energy. My usual picture taking became minimal as I needed to concentrate on each step. Sweat trickled down my back in the ten-degree temperature. I removed my puffy coat and stuffed it into my pack. A green sign poked out of the snow pointing to a spur trail leading to the Stone Elephant, a massive boulder supposedly shaped like its namesake. If the trail wasn't covered in snow, it would have been an interesting detour. But I had no interest in anything except taking the next step.

I made it to the Bald Bluff overlook by lunchtime. The morning had been too cold to bother making a sandwich so I had tossed the squatty plastic jar of cashew butter into my pack. I sat on a bench in the winter sunshine, eating scoops of cashew butter and cheese cubes. Noon, my phone said. I still had nine miles of snow plodding left.

I faced more of the same up and down on the Blackhawk segment. Despite the Aleve I had taken that morning, the bones in my legs throbbed. I started doing my squatting position to bring relief, imagining droplets of pain being squeezed away as my legs folded together. To take my mind off the pain, I thought up a poem about the Flowing Well and Adam Channing.

"What rhymes with Channing? What rhymes with Well?" I tossed out my ideas to the bare trees and came up with my final poem.

Good ol' Adam dug a well,
How deep he'd go, he could not tell.
The water flowed and did not stop.
The town's folk came to not waste a drop.
So if you're hiking with piss-poor planning.
You'll have water thanks to Adam Channing.

Reciting that poem over and over again helped propel me forward. "Good ol' Adam dug a well…" I chanted it like a military cadence with each step. Almost nine hours had passed since Matt dropped me off. Nine hours of battling fresh, deep snow that weekend warriors hadn't had a chance to pack down. Hill after hill. One mountain climb would have been better than the never-ending up and down. At least there would have been a definite end. My concentration waned and my poem chanting fell silent. All I could focus on was my throbbing legs and eventually I stopped feeling them. My feet grew too heavy to lift out of the snow anymore. Numbness took over my mind and body. Fiona was still a mile away.

SQUATTER

Falling onto my knees, I sank into the snow. And sat there. Still and spent. I had nothing left. Minutes ticked by. A squirrel dashed over a snow-covered log. He was in a different world, one that was outside of the fuzzy bubble I currently occupied. Bare tree branches swayed in the breeze creating dancing snow shadows. Their hypnotic dance eased me into a trance. I could fall asleep right here on the trail…right now…just for a few minutes, I thought. Two entwined trees rubbed together creating an eerie creak that echoed through the woods. My breathing slowed; its gentle rhythm lulled me into a stupor. It felt so good to be still. The long afternoon shadows faded. It would soon be dark. Just a little rest for a few more minutes. My body heat melted the snow, and the cool wetness crept through my winter pants. That's okay. I just wanted to be still.

Ding. The familiar sound jolted me out of the fuzzy bubble. I reached into my pocket. It was Matt.

Did your hike go okay? I'm thinking you should be done.

Of course I should be done. It's 5:15, I've been out here all damn day.

Almost done, I texted back.

My damp knees chilled me. "Ouch!" I said as pain seared through my frozen knees. I shivered and dug out my puffy coat from my pack. What am I doing out here? Why am I putting myself through this? Is this accomplishing anything, I wondered. I could keep running, hiding out on the trail, but Mitch would still be there. It had been four months since he screamed at me in my front yard, and I finally let him go. In those four months, I had made my intentions clear that it was over with my short, to-the-point statements. That should be good, right? If I needed help or intervention, four months of asking him to stop should be good. An officer hopefully wouldn't look at me and say, "Now how many times have you gone back?" It was time for true no contact. Not a single word. It was time, dammit.

GET UP, I told myself. You gotta keep moving. STAND. UP. I took a deep breath, stuck my hiking pole into the snow and hauled my stiff body upright. Good. Now walk. "Good ol' Adam dug a well..." I chanted to encourage each step that my body deeply resisted. And then I saw it. Another hill. I couldn't do another one.

"FUUUUCK!!" I yelled as if my wrath would magically flatten it. I reluctantly stepped forward to face the punishment of another incline. A post with a yellow blaze stood guarding the foot of the hill. I squinted. Something else was on the post. Was I seeing it correctly? Could it really be? Underneath the blaze, an arrow pointed to the left. Around the hill.

"I don't hafta go over the hi-ll, the hi-ll, the hi-ll," I sang to a made-up melody. Giddy with excitement and renewed energy I flew through the last mile of the dimly lit woods until Fiona's silhouette came into view. "It's about time," I swear she mumbled.

"Oh Fiona, take me to a cheeseburger," I uttered, and pulled out my phone to text Matt.

Got back to the truck. Dang, a challenging day.

Part Three

I dreamt that I found a snake in my house. It wasn't a rattlesnake and I don't remember it being a particular color. I opened the front door and it left. I found it again. I opened the door and it left. This repeated a few times until the snake never returned.

21

*Suffering and sadness touches us all,
no matter where we fall on the economic ladder.*

A February cold snap arrived, along with a Valentine's Day card, more daily emails, and an audio of Mitch reciting a poem. I replied with my final, clear statement: *Stop emailing and sending cards.*

Temperatures dropped to -20°F and never rose above zero. Doable hiking weather with the right clothing, but sleeping in garages and meals on the tailgate at that temperature was more than I wanted to endure. I took a day to meet up with a couple of hikers from the Facebook group that needed to complete sections next door in Langlade County. On a -15°F degree morning, three strangers met on a road in the woods of northern Wisconsin because of a shared love for the trail.

Meeting people from the trail group was like meeting up with friends. Everyone in the group had the same goal of becoming a Thousand Miler. I met Mark and Jeff at the Highland Lakes trailhead. Other than guessing they were in their fifties and sixties, I couldn't tell much else through the layered bundles. We piled into Jeff's white pickup to shuttle to the other trailhead. We set a fast pace in the bitter cold.

SQUATTER

"Are your feet freezing?" I asked a few minutes into our hike. They both concurred. A good thirty minutes later we generated enough heat that chased away the cold.

"I live in Montello so let me know if you want shuttle rides or a hiking partner to finish the bifurcation," Jeff offered when he heard I still had bifurcation miles to finish.

"For sure. We definitely can share some miles," I said. We conversed a bit more before spacing apart so each could savor nature at her most extreme. That extremeness created a stark, still world. A pure world where the icy air eliminated anything destructive, leaving only goodness to await spring.

Breaks needed to be kept short in the frigid temperature. "Want some chocolate–I always bring chocolate," Mark offered as he dug through his pack. Jeff and I politely declined as we munched on our own snacks but exchanged a quick glance, making me wonder if he was taking the same mental note I was...that if Mark, the chocolate guy, needed a hiking partner in the future, I'd definitely consider it.

* * *

When normal winter temperatures resumed, I completed the bifurcation in four day-trips, with many of the miles hiked with Jeff. I don't remember the specifics of those days other than, as I experienced with Alan in Nevada, Jeff's company being refreshing. Easy-going, male company that didn't cause me stress or anxiety. Jeff was a fellow Gen-Xer and a home inspector whose house was created from a pole building. I found that intriguing. My late husband used to say we should have lived in a quonset hut. My younger self thought that was an outlandish idea. Especially during the nineties when many of my peers lived in gorgeous McMansions. I couldn't fathom the thought of living in something so unconventional. But now, alternative housing fascinates me.

With the bifurcation done and a new friendship solidified, I returned to the southern portion of the state to continue moving toward the Eastern Terminus.

On a late February morning, I began the three-hour drive south under a pre-dawn, cloudy-bright sky. Living in a snowy place allows for the phenomenon where snow reflects light into the night sky and the clouds reflect it back. Illuminating the night as if it were day. Not being a scientist, that's my best explanation.

Robyn, my previous garage host, shuttled me for a road walk. The morning air held a winter chill, but the sun warmed my face, promising the day would unfold into a glorious, February afternoon. The kind of afternoon hardy Wisconsinites yearned for as winter dragged on. The time of year when the sun left its winter resting place low on the horizon to shine brightly, giving warm kisses to a sleeping winter world.

Melting snow poured from the eaves of houses I passed. Mounds of snow along the road receded, creating miniature rivers along the pavement and revealing months' worth of road dirt left behind by plows. I came to the wildly popular Scuppernong segment. For those in the southeastern part of the state, that was the segment to hike. At least, that's what I gathered from Facebook posts. The woods of Scuppernong were revered, and I looked forward to it. Leaving the road for the trail, I plodded through the heavy, wet snow of a field before it led into the woods.

My excitement of finally getting to Scuppernong was squelched. By dog shit. Of course a popular segment would be frequented by lots of people…and their dogs. People who believed that Fido's steaming pile of poo simply vanished in the snow. The snow claimed it, erasing the deed, until winter receded, revealing its shitty secrets. Endless piles of dog shit, thawing in the sunshine, lined the trail. Hints of the warming poo wafted in the breeze. The abundant piles forced me to keep my eyes riveted on the trail to avoid stepping in it. That is my unfortunate memory of the beloved Scuppernong segment.

After finishing the canine excrement caper, the Eagle segment welcomed me as the afternoon warmed. I came to a rocky hill with a sign at its base. An outcropping of rocks named Brady's Rocks. *An Irish immigrant by the name of Michael Brady lived here in 1855 with his wife, Kathleen. They had six children and lived in a 12'x12' log cabin. Mr. Brady quarried stone here...* That sounded like hard physical labor for both Michael and Kathleen. When my kids got the throw-ups in the middle of the night, it was pretty darn convenient to have access to a washing machine. Even though I didn't quarry stone, the ease of opening a box of macaroni and cheese was often welcomed after a hard day.

The internet said that the Ottawa campground in the Kettle Moraine State Forest had some plowed sites. I pulled in. As expected, the ranger station was closed. I had a state park sticker, but not a reservation. The sites weren't cleared out, but the snow had been pushed back enough to park a camper. I had set up my tent on the packed snow in front of Fiona and was gathering up my bedding when a camper rumbled up the road. It stopped, and its window rolled down, revealing a gray-haired couple.

"You gonna sleep in that itty-bitty tent?" the man asked.

"It's gonna be in the twenties tonight," offered the lady, her voice pitching upwards in concern.

"Plenty of room. We're used to the cold." I'd gotten in the habit of sometimes saying "we" to avoid letting people know I was alone. Not that the couple would harm me, but they could unknowingly talk about "that lady camping alone," to the wrong person. They waved and drove away.

With my arms full of bedding, I took a dive next to Fiona's front tire. The thing about a warm day that melted the top layers of snow was that it refroze into a slick glaze after the sun went down. "Damn." I rubbed my shocked rump. I shoulda been wearing my spikes, I thought.

The nearly full moon bathed the forest in light. The refrozen blanket of snow glistened under the brilliant night sky. While that wasn't my first time sleeping out in the cold, it was however, my first time sleeping directly on snow. I had a footprint underneath the tent, a Thermarest inflatable sleeping pad and my vast array of sleeping gear that Fiona lugged around for me. Snuggling in my bags with my water bottle and phone, I soon grew warm. But as the night wore on, the cold seeped up from beneath me. I tried to sleep on my side instead of my back to keep less body surface from touching the pad. But laying on my side for too long made my hips ache.

Is this night over yet? I thought and dug out my phone from my balled up puffy jacket in the sleeping bag with me. It was five. I crawled out of the tent, crept across the ice, and cranked up Fiona. I sat in the driver's seat for a bit, listening to NPR's Morning Edition. Their familiar voices comforted me in the morning darkness. I enjoyed the solo journey, but there were times when human connection was welcomed, even if it was a stranger on the radio.

I didn't bike shuttle that day. My shuttle ride would meet me at the trailhead parking in a higher-end neighborhood at the edge of Delafield. Morning dog walkers stared at my Jetboil perched on the tailgate. My bike lay in a heap in the

SQUATTER

truck bed instead of being propped on a nice bike rack. The walkers politely nodded as they passed.

A young guy from the Facebook group, along with his dog, dropped me off for the day. Frozen footprints of previous hikers dotted the late winter trail, making the terrain uneven and difficult to navigate. My feet twisted and turned with every step. The warm sunshine pushed the temperature into the forties and drove me to shed my jacket.

Up ahead, I saw the stairway built into the side of a hill that led to the Lapham Peak tower. The packed snow on the long stairway had gone through the freeze/melt/refreeze cycle creating an ice slide. No problem. That's why I carried my spikes. I sat down on a log, dug them out of my pack and tried to pull them on. They wouldn't stretch over my boots. My new winter hiking boots. What the heck? They were the same size as both my other boots. But my new boots had thicker, wider soles. Damnit.

I climbed the stairway holding on to the rail while stepping along the edge of the ice slide, taking advantage of the traction from the chunky snow. At the top of the stairway stood the forty-five-foot observation tower offering views of the surrounding Kettle Moraine Forest. I approached the tower's base which was wrapped in orange safety fencing, blocking access to the climb. A sign of the times.

The late-winter day was a battle of the seasons. The air temperature said spring, but the snow-covered ground said winter. The woods opened into a rolling prairie. I passed a bench dedicated to two brothers who died in their twenties, one year apart. The inscription read, *You brought smiles, joy, and richness into our lives. Forever you will be our loving sons.* I Googled their names and was instantly flooded with guilt. Had I invaded their privacy? I took a breath. No, their names were on a public bench in a busy park and they obviously had a story that would arouse curiosity. The unimaginable pain those parents experienced weighed on my mind for the next hour. Hopefully, a pain that I would never know.

It was only mid-afternoon when I returned to Fiona. Over a lunch of dehydrated chicken-fried rice, I contemplated my next move. I rode my bike through Delafield, locked it to a light pole in a shopping center lot and stepped onto the trail that followed along the backside of the shopping center.

Urban segments made bathroom breaks more strategic. Part of the Delafield segment doubled up with the Lake County Recreational Trail. Since the trail was in town, dropping my drawers just anywhere wasn't going to work. I entered a clump of brushy trees that lined the trail and sunk into snow up to my hips. At least I wouldn't have to squat.

Upscale shops and quaint street lamps lined Delafield's streets. The town exuded charm and was meticulously kept. Each building's earth-tone color complemented its neighbor. There were no antiquated cars slumbering in tall weeds waiting for their resurrection day. No crooked rain gutters or handwritten signs advertising nightcrawlers for sale. Not one house with a do-it-yourself paint job done in brilliant green. No sagging chain link fences embedded in narrow strips of high grass where a mower couldn't reach. Delafield was perfect. A perfectly crafted community, thirty-minutes from Milwaukee, offering a quiet sanctuary from the city. A place where high-end shopping could be done, followed by a meal in the company of others who also came to immerse themselves in an elegant, small-town vibe that was minus the small-town problems.

I would spend the next two nights in a garage at the edge of Delafield. Mike, from the Facebook group, had responded

SQUATTER

to my request for shelter. *Hey! My brother lives in Delafield and said you are welcome to stay in their garage*, he wrote. After loading up the old Schwinn from the light pole, I sat in the vast parking lot and thought about dinner. I'd eaten one of my dried meals for lunch. Google said there was a Mobil convenience store in downtown Delafield.

I drove through downtown and didn't see the Mobil station. Google said it was right here. I was looking for what I expected a convenience store to be. A straightforward, plain building set behind a row of gas pumps. Practical. Everyone knows what to expect. Need gas? Wanna coffee and a donut? They've got you covered. Swinging by for a carton of cigarettes? A can of Skoal? A Dew and a Moon Pie? Also check. There was nothing but elegant, earth-colored buildings trimmed in white.

Then I saw it. The familiar Mobil logo with a red O set on the roof. The only gas pump was a vintage red one that greeted customers passing through the white pillars framing the front door. I guessed that the mundane activity of pumping gas didn't mesh with shopping for premium olive oil or fancy wine. I purchased a beautiful chicken salad from an array of selections, a slice of cheesecake that was many notches up from Sara Lee and a kombucha. I followed Google's directions to the address of my garage home for the next two nights.

I pulled into the driveway of my new hosts. In addition to the attached garage, there was a second two-car garage on the property. Nearly the size of my house. The owner pointed me toward the second garage. At a social distance, the fit, professional-looking man introduced himself as Steve.

"Hi, I'm Yolanda," I said while handing him a jar of maple syrup and then stepping back.

"My brother told me there was a hiker looking to stay in a garage and asked if we'd be willing. I thought it was too unusual of a thing to pass up," he said, and then asked about the logistics of how one goes about sleeping in a garage.

"I have a cot that keeps me off of the cement floor."

"Would you like a space heater?"

"Oh no, that's okay, thanks anyway," I said, wanting to be the least intrusive garage guest possible.

When he insisted, I graciously accepted. He returned with a small space heater and a desk lamp to set alongside my cot. "When you're ready, come up to the house and I'll show you the bathroom. You can help yourself to the cookies cooling on the counter." I was dumbstruck by the generosity shown to me, a complete stranger.

Sitting on the cot in front of the little space heater, I ate my dinner from the fancy convenience store. In the morning, Jeannie from the group would meet me in the Delafield shopping center where I had left my bike earlier.

Steve said it would be okay if I left my cot set up in the garage. As a natural early riser, I had plenty of time to kill before meeting Jeannie at eight. I Googled coffee shops near me. Blue Collar Coffee in downtown Delafield popped up. Two minutes away. The shop's name made me think there's a desire to feel connected to the blue-collar roots that ground many family trees. There's a sense of accomplishment that comes with physical labor. Whether it's chopping wood, rebuilding a car engine, riding an elevator down a mine shaft, or driving a semi across the country, there's an intimate connection to work that is completed as a result of one's physical labor.

I parked Fiona in front of Blue Collar Coffee, where she looked appropriately at ease. A chalkboard sign near the

SQUATTER

door read *Cinnamon Rolls*. The interior's worn hardwood floors and corrugated metal walls were the appropriate surroundings in which to start my day after spending the night in a garage. After leaving with my goodies, I parked around the corner to enjoy the hot coffee and warm cinnamon roll. Curious ducks waddled past. I didn't share my cinnamon roll with them.

Jeannie was my ride to the trailhead. She greeted me with a warm, maskless smile as we both had been vaccinated. She and her husband, David, were Thousand Milers, having completed section-hiking the trail in 2014. The trail would lead me near their home the following night.

"We'd love to have you stay with us, and we'll plan a nice dinner," Jeannie offered. I gratefully accepted. "See you tomorrow," she waved as I stepped out of her car.

I entered the snowy woods under a bright, blue sky. The forest, filled with mature maples, was named in honor of Carl Schurz, who was US Secretary of the Interior from 1877 to 1881. His efforts helped pave the way for the creation of the National Park Service, which oversees the Ice Age Trail. I exited the trail onto a road and saw the bridge. The bridge. The arched, concrete, railroad bridge, covered in graffiti that I'd seen posted a gazillion times by hikers. I had passed the 900-mile mark that morning and celebrated by doing an immature, trying-to-be-cool selfie photo shoot in front of the graffiti bridge.

Not only was it a day of reaching 900 miles and seeing the cool bridge, but the temperature topped out at fifty degrees. The first fifty-degree day of the year was a long-anticipated milestone after months where the mercury often didn't rise out of the counting range of a toddler.

By lunchtime, I had left the woods behind and moved through the suburbs of Hartland. Sprawling, manicured lawns were welcome carpets to looming mansions. The snow had receded enough to reveal cement curbs. I sat down on a corner like a wandering vagrant and dug out my lunch.

* * *

That night, I flipped on the little heater and sat on my cot in Steve's Delafield garage. The soft glow from the reading lamp created a cozy bubble that kept away the cold darkness. A tipped-up wheelbarrow, a grill waiting for summer and a snowblower with chained tires loomed in the shadows like creatures waiting to come alive. I could become a connoisseur of garage living. Rating garages for their comfort level. I scrolled through Mitch's daily emails. I stood firm in my no contact. I didn't feel guilty anymore for not responding. Not answering was getting easier.

In the morning, I said goodbye to Delafield after another stop at Blue Collar Coffee and drove north to meet Jeannie again for a shuttle ride. Fog shrouded the world that last February morning, creating a mystical atmosphere for the Holy Hill segment. Holy Hill Basilica and National Shrine of Mary grandly sat atop a 1,350-foot glacial kame. The two majestic steeples that towered over the landscape normally could be seen for miles. But that morning they were concealed in a veil of gray mist. After multiple days of energizing blue sky, the calming fog hid the world beyond my immediate surroundings.

The barely visible Holy Hill trailhead sign stood like a portal entry to an unearthly dimension. The brown sign's yellow lettering stood in stark contrast to the black-and-white world it guarded. The snow-packed trail beyond it vanished into the same gray veil that engulfed the massive basilica. I paused at the sign and smiled as my imagination conjured up a scene where the lost crusader hesitated before entering the unknown dimension. I followed the trail into a mystical world where at any moment magical, wide-eyed creatures could appear from behind the trees. The dense fog created an unnatural silence, interrupted only by my rhythmic, crunching footsteps in the snow.

The miles of the morning passed uneventfully until the joyful ringing of bells pierced the silence and boomed through the fog. Had I unknowingly died on the trail and stood at the misty gates of heaven? Like in movies where the person died and didn't know it. The basilica bells announced throughout the land that it was Sunday noon. I stopped and listened, taking in the magic of the trail.

By afternoon, the fog lifted and left behind drab gray. The recent days of warm sunshine left bare patches of ground exposed. I found a patch of dry pine needles and sat to eat my lunch. While crossing a field on the Loew Lake segment, the distant towers of Holy Hill came into view. When my thirteen miles were complete, I drove up to see the source of the magical bells.

I led Fiona up the winding drive to the top of the kame that was home to the Roman Catholic shrine. Two cars sat in the vast parking lot. Staff maybe? While stepping out of the truck, icy wind slapped me and whipped the door from my hands. Holding tight to my hat, I crossed the parking lot and stood at the base of the looming structure. The internet said that the scenic towers were closed. Signs were posted on the doors. The wind chilled me, so I didn't bother to get close enough to read them. I was sure they said the same thing as everywhere else. The trail brought me past interesting places that I couldn't experience. My mood was reflected in the dirty, melting snow that lined the road leading down the hill. I'm not here to sightsee, I told myself. I'm here to take my life back.

I drove through a neighborhood of tidy suburban homes and pulled into Jeannie and David's driveway. She greeted me at the door, wearing a green pullover that accented her short, stylishly cut hair. "We straightened up the garage, but you are welcome to stay inside. You can choose the guest room or the basement," she said as I handed her a jar of maple syrup.

On the wall of their finished basement hung their giant Thousand Miler Map which was also a checklist of segments. I had the same map and looked longingly at it, thinking that it wouldn't be long before mine was complete. I chose to set up my sleeping bag on the carpeted basement floor.

"I've always dreamed of owning a bed and breakfast after I retired," Jeannie said while stirring a pot of stew. "I love hosting hikers. Would you sign my guestbook?" She left the kitchen and came back with the book. As I signed, a knock at the front door interrupted our conversation. Jeannie answered and said someone was there to see me. Inside the door stood Sanjay from the Facebook group. Born Sakshi Krishna Das in Bombay, India, Sanjay now resided outside of Milwaukee. With the support of his family, he had taken on the challenge of the trail and had recently contacted me asking if we could meet up. Sanjay said he wanted to bring me a gift.

"Nice to finally meet you, Sanjay," I said to the pleasant-looking man with dark hair and glasses that framed a masked face. He held a large paper bag.

"I have some gifts," he said while digging into the bag. "Food prepared by my wife, who's an excellent cook. It's cholay—cooked chickpeas."

SQUATTER

"I love Indian food!" I exclaimed. Lots of time goes into preparing an Indian meal and I was thrilled to be on the receiving end of that effort.

He unwrapped and opened a small container, revealing two brown morsels. Little nuggets of some type. "This is Holy Food," Sanjay explained, intriguing me. Lastly, he handed me a string of light-brown Hindu beads. "Please carry these in your backpack for blessings and protection."

"I will," I assured him. We took fun pictures together and Jeannie invited him to stay for dinner, which he declined as he needed to head home. After placing the food in the truck where it would stay cold until I could share it with Liz and Grace, I sat at Jeannie's table and ate the tiny, Holy morsels. The simple, plain flavor didn't detract from the fact that I partook in something reverent. I felt truly honored that Sanjay had taken time to share the gift of his culture with me.

That night, I placed the beads in my backpack, unaware of how much their blessing would be needed before reaching the end of the trail.

22

There are good people who love this trail.

After visiting my son, John, and his family in Texas, I returned to the trail on the last day of March, ready to slay the final two hundred miles. Grace stayed behind at her brother's for an extended visit, allowing me to spend longer stretches out on the trail. I didn't burden my adult kids with my issue with Mitch. In some ways, I was still in the mindset of parenting younger kids in regard to sharing my problems; kids don't need to be a sounding board for their parents' problems. But in order to fully move from the parent/child relationship into friendship with adult kids, you need to be open and willing to share what's happening in your life. That was something I needed to work on.

Jeff and I planned to hike a couple of days together as he needed to complete some of the segments. We would share a campsite at Mauthe Lake Campground in the Kettle Moraine State Forest.

We left Fiona at a trailhead and drove his white pickup north for a day on the Southern Kewaskum and West Bend segments. Since we would be sharing a campsite, I felt the need to set things straight. Not that Jeff had ever behaved in any way that made me think that he needed to be set straight. He had proved himself a friend. But my life

SQUATTER

In the morning darkness, I stealthily packed up so as not to wake Eric's family or the neighbors. I drove off in search of a McDonald's breakfast sandwich to eat on the way to the Parnell trailhead. While sitting in the drive-thru, the image of Eric's orange extension cord popped into my head. I forgot to roll it up. While packing up in the dark, it had been easy to overlook. I hated the idea of being a sloppy guest. I would make sure to message him an apology at a more appropriate hour.

At the trailhead, I packed a sandwich for lunch and waited for Scott, my shuttle ride. The challenging, fourteen-mile Parnell segment wound through the northern Kettle Moraine State Forest, with a four-mile stretch running atop the Parnell Esker. Scott pulled up. I hopped in and greeted the retired, clean-cut looking man.

"So you're from Wausau. I have a friend in Wausau," said Scott. We made the connection that we knew the same person.

"She used to be my neighbor," I said. We talked about the trail and other small-talk topics. He talked about his life and family.

"My wife and I have a lake house nearby," Scott said. He had a calming presence and told me the story of why they had a lake house seven minutes from their regular home:

"Being a physician before I retired, I spent a lot of time on call and couldn't be far from home. So, we thought instead of a place Up North we'd get a place nearby. We could enjoy the feeling of getting away, but I could still be on call."

Brilliant. I imagined that his warm, peaceful presence extended to a reassuring bedside manner that comforted his patients. "Do you have a place to stay tonight? You're more than welcome to stay at our lake house," he said. Again, a stranger's generosity left me stunned.

"Thank you so much, but I do have a place at a friend's for tonight."

Scott delivered me to the trailhead, and I headed off for a day of endless up and down. Parnell was a popular segment, so I was pleased to have the morning alone. I had been expecting people even on a weekday morning due to the number of photos posted on Facebook. My bladder said it was time for a pee stop. In my overconfidence of being alone, I dropped my pants at the edge of the trail and experienced a hiking first for me. Getting caught with my pants down.

Someone had been gaining on me all morning. In the middle of taking care of business, a guy crested the hill. "Oh gosh, sorry," he mumbled and turned his back.

"I'm sooo sorry," I stuttered and fumbled about, putting myself back together. "Okay!" I called out, trying to regain some level of decorum. He passed me and we exchanged awkward smiles. I dug out my sandwich, allowing him to get farther ahead. No need to create more uncomfortable moments with a random stranger who had just seen my bare butt. I'd been on the other side of this story before. My son, John, and I had been hiking in White Sands, New Mexico. We crested a dune and there stood a naked guy, as gleaming white as the desert sand. At the sight of us, he nonchalantly turned and entered his tent that was perched in the sand.

The hours dragged on. Up ahead the peeing escapade guy sat on a bench overlooking Butler Lake. He saw me and smiled. A brief humorous moment broke the up and down monotony.

"Hey again—this time I've got my pants up." I said, dashing by.

The constant up and down wore on me. If you looked at a map of Wisconsin's forests, it would be top heavy with green touch. A light drizzle continued while I unloaded my bike. Before pedaling off, I confirmed the next day's shuttle ride from Scott, who had driven me to Parnell on my last trip out.

The offer for the lake house still stands, he texted. My plans were to camp at Mauthe Lake. More rain was forecasted, and I was prepared to camp in the rain if I had to. But Scott's offer meant that I didn't have to. I accepted, and he said to text him when I finished with my day.

Sprinkles and gray sky, along with the trail settling into a gentle meander after the Kettle Moraine drama, gave the day a quiet vibe. Not a remote wilderness quiet, but a rural, slower-paced take-a-deep-breath-and-shake-it-off kind of quiet. The misty day painted the world with soft, watercolor hues. The muted colors along the trail also adorned the barns and homes of the road walk. In the coming days, miles of roads, towns or bike paths would replace trails.

I followed the directions to Scott's house on Crystal Lake. He signaled for me to pull into the garage. I stepped out of the truck and noticed the wooden planked garage floor. I had become a connoisseur of garage living. "The garage would be totally fine," I said to Scott after handing him a jar of syrup.

"Absolutely not," replied Scott. "You'll have the house to yourself." He gave me a tour of their second home. Spacious. Gorgeous. Massive glass windows covered the entire side of the house facing the lake. I followed him in awe. Not only of the house, but the fact that someone would trust me with it when they didn't even know me.

Scott's generosity left me speechless. The trail was introducing me to good and generous people. People who shared their land, homes, garages, yards, and time with me. New friends who enjoyed my company. Good people really existed. I needed the trail to remind me of that.

Before he left, I asked Scott if there was a nearby convenience store. "I think I want dessert tonight."

"No, there's nothing nearby," Scott said. After a pause, he opened a cupboard door and pulled out a giant bag of M&Ms. "Here, help yourself." The ultimate generous gesture: sharing your secret stash of chocolate.

I ate a chili mac dinner on the dock overlooking Crystal Lake under heavy gray skies. Rain looked to be moving in. I unrolled my sleeping bag on the couch. Scott said I was welcome to sleep in any of the beds, but I didn't want to disturb anything. By seven o'clock, it was pouring rain; massive thunderclaps rattled the house. As lightning lit up the sky, it illuminated the lake being battered by the deluge. That woulda sucked to be out there drowning in my tent, I thought.

Hot chocolate with the M&Ms sounded like a cozy combination during the storm. I filled a coffee cup with water and searched for the microwave. I couldn't find it. There's no way this house doesn't have a microwave, I thought. I gave up and boiled water on the stove for my hot chocolate. In the morning while making breakfast, I opened a drawer in search of utensils and found the microwave. In a drawer. A magical microwave drawer. I had never seen such a thing. My house was basic. The trail certainly opened up new experiences for me. Even regarding microwaves.

Scott's continued generosity and love for the trail meant he would shuttle me for the next couple of days. We met in the Elkhart Lake Cemetery where I left Fiona. Another day of rain and drizzle. I was okay with that. Most of the day would be road miles, and I wouldn't have to worry about sunburn. I plodded along the wet asphalt in my rain poncho while listening to podcasts on toxic relationships. I monk with a stately white beard and wise eyes came and stood behind the smaller, head table. Of the seven monks that resided there, only four arrived for dinner. We stood behind our chairs and bowed our heads for prayer before the white-bearded monk gave permission for us to fill our plates at the buffet. I approached an array of pastas, salads, and desserts.

"Looks like you've joined us for leftover night," said the white-bearded monk.

"Everything looks wonderful," I said, trying not to over-pile my plate. I was famished.

The monks usually ate their meals in silence. "Tonight, since we have a guest, I will allow conversation," the white-bearded monk announced. The two monks who joined Father Paisius at the table across from me said they were from Australia and Ireland.

"You're hiking a trail that goes through the whole state?" One of the monks asked in a thick Irish accent. He had hiked in Europe and was interested in hearing about the trail.

"We haven't hosted an Ice Age Trail hiker before," said Father Paisius. He talked about the spiritual pilgrimage called the Wisconsin Way, where hikers go from shrine to shrine and often stop at St. Nazianz. Not being Catholic, I hadn't heard of it.

Dinner conversation became relaxed and fun after the stiff formalities of the newly introduced were over. At first glance the monks appeared similar. But as dinner progressed their unique personalities emerged. The funny guy dropped quick-witted statements without missing a beat. The thoughtful one carefully chose his words before speaking. The intellectual one seemed levelheaded and reliable.

The wise one kept everyone in line and did so with a gentle manner.

The meal was over when everyone finished eating. Father Paisius walked me to my room on the second floor.

"So what do you do if a monk wants to join but is a terrible singer?" I joked as we walked down a long hallway on the second floor. The funny monk's antics had rubbed off on me during dinner.

Father Paisius paused thoughtfully before answering. "Well...the other monks must endure the bad singing and hope that he improves." That right there is all that's needed to get through life. Endurance and hope.

"You'll be the only one on this floor," Father Paisius said. "We live on the third floor which is off-limits to guests."

He said goodnight and walked down the dark hallway. I entered the simple, yet charming room. A twin bed, a nightstand, and a sink, with a bathroom across the hall. Everything needed for basic comfort. I glanced through the sheer curtains. Fiona sat parked at the edge of the sprawling lawn. I took a bath and soaked for a while. The pipes in the wall rattled whenever water got turned on in another part of the old building. I snuggled in my bed as nighttime prayers were broadcast over the hallway's speaker. The sacred melody led me into a peaceful sleep.

Bells gonged over the speaker at six o'clock announcing that morning prayers would soon begin. I got ready for the day to the sound of chanting. The night before, Father Paisius showed me the sanctuary's balcony that was down the hall from my room. I crept through the balcony door and sat down. It wasn't like a regular church balcony that offered a view while seated. I longed for an image of the sanctuary. But I didn't want to be intrusive by peeking over

SQUATTER

The delicate nun led me to a small library just inside the doors.

"You can wait here," she said, and left the room.

She returned with a middle-aged-looking nun who emitted the energy of someone who had a busy schedule and ran a tight ship. I stood to greet her. "I'm Sister Carmen Marie," she stated. "Why didn't you text me when you arrived? You did not follow my instructions."

"Ummm…" I stammered, standing there with my mouth open, which instantly became parched. Thankfully, the mask somewhat hid my embarrassment. I was certain I followed her instructions. But apparently, I flubbed up.

"You're lucky that someone was here to answer the door. You could have been left out there," she gestured toward the window. Her voice softened. "Now where did you park?"

"Ummm, out front?" My voice rose as if asking a question, because now I was uncertain if I had done anything correctly.

"Very good. I will ride with you back to the cottage."

She followed me outside and down the grand stairs to where Fiona sat in the lot. I would not be staying inside the vast, historic Mother House. As we wound our way to the backside of the campus property, she told me about the convent that housed over one hundred nuns.

"The average age of our nuns is seventy-eight. Women aren't choosing this life anymore," she said, shaking her head. We passed a separate, more modern building. "That's our college. We had to close for Covid. That hurt us so badly that we will not be able to reopen."

I listened to her speak and felt her sadness as she recalled a lifestyle that she viewed as dying. She pointed to a quaint cottage ahead. "That's it. You can pull up next to it."

26

*Mitch had to have scoured the internet
looking for a woman he thought was me.*

The day after my birthday, I tended to household chores and unloaded Fiona before a work stretch. The house was quiet, with Grace still in Texas and Liz at work. I folded laundry in the basement and heard a faint knock on the kitchen door. I paused.

Nothing.

Maybe I imagined it. I finished folding towels and climbed the stairs carrying the laundry basket. The inside kitchen door was open, over the basement stairs, as I had been unloading my gear throughout the morning. The familiar white sleeve of the button down shirt Mitch wore to court reached across the door's square windows. His knuckles tapped the glass. I stomped up the rest of the stairs, swung the door out of my way and tossed the laundry basket onto the kitchen floor. Mitch retreated back into the driveway. I opened the screen door.

"You need to leave. I don't want to see you," I said. Without waiting for a response, I closed and locked the door. I'd worked too hard and had come too far to get sucked back in.

He didn't leave. Instead, he sat on my porch and pulled out his phone.

I parked Fiona for a road walk. I pedaled my Schwinn, battling the wind. After fifty minutes of heavy pedaling, I had biked the seven miles to where I left off the day before. The relentless wind repeatedly blew down my hood. I took my winter headband and put it on the outside of the hood, hoping that would secure it. It was a ridiculous look, but I couldn't take the wind battering my head. Plus, I was trying to listen to a podcast.

I had learned a plethora of information about psychological abuse. My eyes opened to the fact that I had been influenced by psychological tactics of control and manipulation. I didn't fully understand why I was drawn in, but learned that a person like Mitch and a person like me mixed together made for the perfect storm.

For the drive home, OneRepublic's song, "Good Life," thumped from Fiona's speakers on repeat. While driving the backcountry roads, I spotted something perched on a fence post.

A bald eagle. Was it fake? It had to be.

I stopped at the side of the road and rolled down the window to see if the bird was one of those realistic wood carvings sold at art fairs. The eagle turned its head and stared at me. My mouth fell open at its majestic presence. The eagle's piercing gaze struck me as we made eye contact. I was open to the idea that God speaks to us through nature, whether through dreams or real life. Some believe that an eagle makes an appearance to let you know it's time to be courageous because a challenge is headed your way.

SQUATTER

A woman with a deep, smoker's voice told about a run-in she had with a "smart-mouthed kid" while shopping. "If dat was my grandson–I'da backhanded 'em."

Not only did Connie know the customers, the customers knew each other. An older gentleman stood at the counter waiting for his to-go order. A woman sitting at the counter greeted him. "How's your stones, Irvin? Did they blast 'em?"

I ate my BLT, left a good tip, and drove out of town with the memories of Connie's diner where people listened to each other's rants of the day, their long-winded family history and even inquired about kidney stones.

* * *

The eighth and final day out for that trip was my fifty-third birthday. In an email, Mitch said he wanted to see me for my birthday. No contact. And I'd been sticking to it. I didn't respond. I lounged around in my tent until well after sunrise before rolling out of my bag and heading to the beach parking lot for breakfast overlooking Lake Michigan. The rough and choppy lake indicated it would be another windy, gray day.

Last year, I spent my birthday on a segment near home with less than fifty trail miles logged. This year, I would spend my birthday on the trail with less than fifty miles to finish. I was almost done. My hike on the Ice Age Trail would soon be over. I would never relive this exact experience again. Even if I did the trail a second time, it wouldn't be during the first year of Covid when the world was uncertain. I wouldn't meet masked strangers who let me sleep in their cold garages. I might not hear wolves howl or wake up to the first October snow.

My oatmeal got hard to swallow.

Even stranger than the messages were the red, smiley faces dotted throughout the words. Were they enticing smiles from a killer clown hoping to lure its victim? Were bodies hidden in the ruins of the once-happy homestead? I imagined a crazed-looking character with rotting teeth being the perpetrator of such graffiti. Crazed clowns and serial killers were definitely scary, but what's scarier was that the normal-looking, friendly guy who helped snow-blow his neighbor's sidewalk might be the writer of the blood-red words and creepy smiley faces. I walked my pants-wearing-self right past that old place, but not without a few glances behind me. Because Wisconsin has produced its share of deranged murderers.

* * *

Before driving to Point Beach for the night, I stopped at Connie's Diner in Two Rivers and took a seat at one of the ten stools along the counter.

"Can I get you something to drink?" asked a young lady through a bandana covering her face. I craved a Pepsi after the long road walk.

The small diner consisted of four booths and two tables. Other customers addressed a stout lady behind the counter, who looked to be near retirement age, as Connie. While wearing shorts, black compression socks and practical shoes, Connie served up dinners and greeted her regular customers by name. Conversations swirled around the cozy diner.

A lady in a purple sweater explained in detail how her great aunt died of bladder cancer.

Someone in a booth ranted about a broken soda machine she encountered earlier in the day. "I lost three quarters!"

SQUATTER

* * *

Much of the trail in those last hundred miles would either be road walking, urban segments or along rail/trail. Reaching the end was a matter of ticking off the easy miles. I enjoyed ninety-minutes lollygagging on a two-mile stretch of trail that followed along the beach of Lake Michigan. Fog rolled in from the lake and crept up the dunes. The sun broke through the clouds. The mix of sunbeams, dark rain clouds and rolling fog was a photographer's playground. After two nights at the convent, the empty Point Beach State Park would be home for a couple of nights.

On a seventeen-mile road walk, I endured hours of wind. The day could be summed up with two words: gray and long. I approached an abandoned farmstead, stripped of all color after withering in the sun and suffering years of neglect. The small barn's roof sagged in the middle. One outbuilding leaned to the left, yielding to the overgrown, bare vines attempting to claim it back to the land. Forgotten, colorless farmsteads were common to Wisconsin's landscapes. But this one was unique. Messages painted in crude, blood-red lettering were plastered over every available space. Messages intended for the lost.

God Have Mercy.
Dress Modestly Pray.
Men Wear Pants.
Jesus Loves Modesty.
God Almighty-We Love You Mary-Must Holy Pray for Us Sinners.
Modesty God.
Holy Angel Keep Me From Hell.

The simple, wooden frame cottage bore the name St. Anne Hall and sat amidst the convent gardens overlooking Silver Lake. We climbed the steps to enter the three-season porch. Sister Carmen Marie dug out a key from her pocket and opened the door to the people-sized dollhouse, consisting of a bedroom, a living room and a bath. She handed me the cottage key, which I promptly added to my key ring. There was no way I was losing that key. She gave me specific check-out instructions. I repeated them back to her to ensure accuracy. I would not disappoint Sister Carmen Marie again. I walked out with her and went to Fiona to grab a gallon jug of maple syrup.

"Thank you so much for allowing me to stay and again, I apologize for the mix up," I said. She gave an understanding smile and I watched her walk toward the Mother House with the maple syrup jug tucked under her arm. Left to myself, I passed the time exploring the historic grounds. Wandering the cemetery, I marveled at the women who had given their lives to service.

I took a shower and sat in the miniature living room with a Kwik Trip convenience store salad and kombucha for dinner. I turned on the TV, curled my legs underneath me and found The Golden Girls. I knew it would be sweet sailing after leaving the Kettle Moraine, but enjoying the comfy surroundings while watching TV felt a bit like cheating. After so many nights of sleeping in my tent or garages, my recent cozy accommodations felt odd. The adventure was almost over. Nothing wrong with it being a little easy. I had earned easy. I smiled along with Blanche and Rose, and finished dinner.

I knew he was emailing me. I checked my spam folder. Sure enough. He sent a photo of a silhouetted man and woman watching a sunset. The woman wore a baseball cap with her hair pulled through the back, just like I did. Her head was slightly turned so that you could see she wore glasses. Just like me. A closer look revealed that her face was rounder than mine. But Mitch saw what he wanted to see. And he saw 'me' in that photo with another man.

To make sure there were no misunderstandings and that my message was clear, I opened the front door.

"If you don't leave, I will call the police and get a restraining order if I have to." He smirked. To him, this was a game. I closed the door without allowing a response.

He continued to sit on my porch, oozing his I'm-above-the-law arrogance.

10:52 email: *I want to ask you about this photo, that's all.*

I dialed 911. "My ex-fiancé won't leave my front porch."

10:55: *why couldn't you just be honest with me so I could have moved on a long time ago.*

"No, I don't believe he has any weapons."

10:58: *I just want to know why you broke our exclusive physical intimacy because I have never done that.*

"I've been trying to end the relationship, but he won't let go."

Two officers walked up the street and crossed my front yard. One talked with Mitch outside and the other joined me in the kitchen.

"This will sound strange, but it's almost like he's become a stalker," I said to the officer.

"Stalkers are often an ex-partner," the officer said. "That can make it difficult for the victim to see what's happening since it's someone she knows and the behavior has become familiar."

SQUATTER

Oh my gosh. He nailed it. That was exactly how I felt. Mitch's behavior was indeed familiar, and I had normalized it. Something I lived with every day.

The officer took my concerns seriously and mentioned a restraining order.

"He's an attorney and that concerns me. He has the upper hand," I said.

"His behavior is unacceptable and you'd be assigned an out-of-county judge," the officer said.

The other officer came in after speaking with Mitch.

"He did admit that you told him to leave," the other officer said. "He's been instructed not to have contact with you again."

The emails stopped. But I knew Mitch. It would only be a matter of time.

* * *

After a work stretch, I returned to the trail for three days. I could have easily finished the trail in four, but I wanted to share my last day with those of my kids who were able to come. Grace was in Texas until early May. I set a finish date of Saturday, May 15. Three of my five kids and one grandchild would be able to share the day with me. A crisp, blue sky welcomed me back to eastern Wisconsin. A welcome change from the persistent gloom of the last trip out. My shuttle ride drove me into Kewaunee. The Kewaunee River segment was rail/trail that ran twelve-and-a-half miles along the Ahnapee State Trail. The segment began at the foot of a giant grandfather clock.

The roadside attraction stood nearly thirty-six feet tall, making it the World's Tallest Grandfather Clock. And it worked. Chiming every quarter hour. It was built in 1976, as a gimmick to promote a local business and attract tourists to Kewaunee. The clock was abandoned after the business closed, but was revived, restored, and moved to the Ahnapee/Ice Age Trail trailhead in the center of town.

I turned on a podcast and strolled for hours in the sunshine along the flat rail/trail. I learned new terms for my experiences: love bombing, gaslighting, projection, trauma bonds, smear campaigns, narcissism, highly sensitive people.

I had trouble grasping it all. Those things happen to other people. People on those dramatic news shows. They happened in the movies. Not in small-town Wisconsin. But it was all coming together. I knew I had a long way to go and more to discover about myself. But during my time on the trail, I had done what I set out to do: I had broken my addiction to Mitch.

* * *

It was only mid-afternoon, and I wanted to poke around Kewaunee. I hadn't been to the little towns in that area that dotted the Lake Michigan shoreline. Quaint Norman Rockwell towns with more of a New England feel than Midwestern.

I had traveled to all parts of the state, so I thought I knew Wisconsin. But the trail showed me that I really didn't know Wisconsin well at all. On all our homeschool field trips to Madison or Milwaukee when the kids were growing up, we'd pass signs for towns like Lodi, Cross Plains, Monticello, and Delafield. They were random names on the way to our destination. But the trail took me to those places.

I wanted to visit Kewaunee's Jail Museum, but it was closed. The old Tug Ludington from World War II floated in the harbor waiting for tours to resume in May. The town slept during its quiet off-season. With the promise of summer, towns everywhere hoped to spring back to life and dust away the cobwebs after a year of Covid.

    I fell asleep in my tent at Point Beach State Park listening to Lake Michigan pound the shore under a bright moon. In the dark morning, I once again had breakfast in the parking lot and watched the day arrive. I witnessed many sunrises over the last year and my chest grew heavy at the thought that it would be one of the last sunrises of my trail adventure. The year was almost over. My mission of letting go of Mitch was successful. But then what? What happens after dedicating a year to something so big?

* * *

I leapfrogged to complete the long road walk into Algoma. I could take my time. Only a handful of miles left to complete the trail. During the road walk along Highway 42, I pondered where to stay the night. Earlier, I had eaten a second breakfast at Kunkel's diner in Kewaunee after my first bike/hike.

    "Do you know of any off-season camping or property where I might be able to pitch a tent for the night?" I asked my server. I was too far north from Point Beach State Park to make that a reasonable option.

    "I haven't lived here long, but I'll think on it," she answered. I zoomed in on Google looking for anything: a church, school, business, any place I might be able to pitch a tent. I left Kunkel's with a full belly, but empty of ideas for the night.

* * *

I pedaled through Algoma on my final bike shuttle of the day and approached the Forestville segment trailhead, which was also part of the Ahnapee State Trail. A police car sat in the large lot. A really large lot with enough space to conspicuously pitch a tent in the corner. Tucked in the back of the lot loomed a large electric grid surrounded by fencing. This is my chance, I thought. I could sleep here. I pedaled up the officer's car. He rolled down the window.

"Hello!" I said, maybe a tad too bright and smiley. He looked like a cranky, old grandpa who wanted nothing but peace and quiet. "I'm hiking the Ice Age Trail…and bike-shuttling myself," I added to explain why I was on a bike after just saying I was hiking. "I'll be doing this segment early tomorrow morning, so I'm wondering if it would be okay if I parked here overnight and pitched a tent…ah…maybe back behind that electric grid? No one would see me." I nodded in the grid's direction. And smiled.

"That's property of the electric company," he said matter-of-factly. I was certain I had interrupted the few quiet moments he hoped to get in his day. I needed more pep.

"Ohhh…okay…ummm…but I'd arrive after dark and leave before sunrise. And I won't touch anything," I smiled.

"Welllll…"

I smiled bigger.

"Allll right, go ahead," he caved like a grandpa with a grouchy facade but still had a heart that couldn't say no. "Stay behind there," he said flatly and tossed his head in the direction of the grid, "I'll let the night shift know you're there."

"Awesome! Thank you so much!" I locked up my bike and walked back through Algoma to where Fiona was parked at the Highway 42 wayside outside of town.

Algoma had gone through a few name changes over the years. In 1851, the settlement was named Wolf River Trading Post. Eight years later, it was changed to Ahnepee after a Potawatomi legend. People constantly misspelled the town's name, using an "a" in the middle instead of an "e". The town decided to change the spelling to what people were doing anyway, so it went from Ahnepee to Ahnapee. That name didn't stick either after the town's residents were being called Ahnapeepers. Anna was a popular girl's name in the late 1800s. The joke of being called 'Anna peepers' didn't sit well with the residents. They searched for a new name and decided on Algoma, a Pottawatomie word meaning Park of Flowers. With it being April, I couldn't discern whether the name was an accurate description.

I walked out of Algoma along Highway 42. Clouds had stolen the blue sky. A steady Lake Michigan breeze was enough to warrant wearing a banana around my neck. With the arrival of milder spring weather, I had traded my heavy winter gaiter and headband for a bandana and a brimmed sun hat.

In the distance, black smoke rose above the treeline. Maybe someone's burning brush, or it's a garage fire, I thought. The smoke rose higher into the sky. Geez, that's some fire. But something wasn't right. The smoke didn't move like smoke. "What the hell?" The dark form billowed into the sky, towering above Highway 42.

Birds?

No.

Bugs.

Out of the heavens came The Great Algoma Plague of '21. The entire black form twisted in unison and spiraled downward.

Toward me.

The swarm swooped down like a black tentacle preparing to wrap itself around its victim. I stopped on the highway's shoulder, covered my face with the bandana, held my breath and squeezed my eyes shut.

So this is how it ends, I thought. Tomorrow's headline will read…*Unfortunate Hiker Taken Down on Highway 42 by Great Algoma Plague.* Within seconds, millions…no…billions of tiny, black bugs engulfed me. They battered my puffy jacket, flew in under my hat's rim and squiggled into my ears. They attempted to squeeze their way around the bandana's edges, but my hands firmly sealed the cloth over my nose and mouth.

And then they were gone. The swarm moved on into Algoma as I brushed off the stragglers left behind that dotted my body. I continued walking and crossed a white cement bridge coated with the bugs. I examined them. Many were stuck together, end to end in a mating ritual, too distracted to keep up with the rest.

Fiona fared pretty well at the wayside. I brushed off the bugs that settled on her blue varnish before opening the door to change into my Crocs. I sat in the front seat and Googled the bugs. They were harmless midges—aquatic insects commonly found near the Great Lakes. It was their mating and hatching season. I debated over my night's plans.

Do I really want to spend one of my last nights on the trail sleeping next to a giant electric grid while midge mayhem is taking place?

But I've managed to do the trail with only one night in a motel. I was hoping to avoid the cost.

I'm not broke so get over it, I thought. Staying in a motel doesn't lessen the experience.

I decided on the River Hills Motel in Algoma with an off-season rate of $69. I arrived for the contactless check-in, and was pleased with my decision. The darling mom and pop place overlooked the Ahnapee River. The rooms lined a deck spanning the length of the motel. I entered my renovated, crisp, and simple room. Its screen door kept me connected to the outside.

After showering, I settled on the bed with my grocery store dinner and watched the world through the screen. The orange sunset silhouetted the bare branches of a giant tree framing the Motel's road sign. Geese, settling in on the river, honked and made various other noises that rose up the river's bank. I made the right choice. At least the night-shift officer wouldn't have to check up on a lady camping behind the electric grid.

The next day's drizzle matched my dark mood. My trail experience was almost over and my heart felt heavy. Off in the distance, an explosion of midges rose above the horizon. Smoke, my ass. You can't fool me twice, I laughed. Well actually, maybe you can.

I drove home in the rain, leaving behind only thirteen miles of the trail to finish. How easily I could stay and complete the miles. The kids were busy with their lives, and they wouldn't have to make the trip across the state. But the day was planned, and I looked forward to sharing it.

I solemnly watched the road through the spattering of raindrops being rhythmically wiped away. My adventure was basically over.

27

The trail is done and I filed a restraining order.

Saturday, May 15, was completion day. I had become accustomed to helping myself to empty, closed campgrounds. It didn't occur to me that Potawatomi State Park would be full on a Saturday in May with people itching for the return of normalcy after a year of Covid. Luckily, Dennis came to the rescue and offered me his place to stay.

Celebration filled the day. I walked the last miles of the Ice Age Trail to the Eastern Terminus with new trail friends from the Facebook group, including Sanjay, who had given me the beads. Three of my five kids and one grandchild made it and met me at the finish. Gifts, cards, congratulations, and a celebration brewery pizza marked the occasion. The kids and I even stopped to tour Tug Ludington, which had opened for the season.

I didn't think tears would come, but they did. I had done this big thing. A big, giant thing. And just like that, it was over. I hadn't done it because I wanted to hike a trail. I had done it because I needed a way to run from Mitch. I had never learned how to create boundaries.

There would be no more running.

SQUATTER

* * *

I sat on my front porch, enjoying morning coffee after the hubbub of the trail finish followed by a couple of twelve-hour shifts. No more packing up for the trail or planning logistics. What now? The loss of the trail weighed on me. I had no place to go and nothing to do. At least nothing big like hiking a National Scenic Trail. The trail had been my life and world for the last year.

I took a sip of coffee and felt compelled to glance at the mailbox mounted next to the front door. Sometimes Liz and Grace didn't grab the mail on my work days, and I hadn't checked it either. Somehow, I knew something from Mitch sat in the mailbox. A weird, pulsating energy emanated from that black box. I flipped open the top and peaked in at a long, white, fat envelope. Mitch's familiar return address sticker was in the upper corner. It had been postmarked May 17.

I pulled out a typed, single-spaced, three-page letter, scanning over it at first. The same twisted shit. Then I actually read it. The photo that he wanted to ask me about…the one that wasn't me…he had created an entire, in-depth scenario around it. The location, when it was taken, how I met this man…on and on…like a deranged, obsessed soul not living in reality. I had lived with that insanity for three-and-a-half years.

It was time to file a restraining order.

* * *

Feeling detached from my surroundings, I handed in the papers at the courthouse on a bright, June day. A flash of surprise, almost imperceivable if I hadn't been watching for it, crossed the clerk's face after seeing Mitch's name. I didn't feel the guilt I had expected for the embarrassment that might cause him. I felt nothing. I simply went through the motions. The clerk snapped back to her stern, down-to-business vibe. I had placed Mitch's emotional comfort over my own needs long enough.

"You can follow me," said the clerk. She led me to a waiting room outside one of the judge's chambers and handed the papers to another clerk sitting behind a desk. I knew the judge. I knew two of the four county judges. Mitch, of course, knew all four.

"Have a seat while the judge reviews this," said clerk #2. When filing a restraining order, a judge either accepts or denies the petition. If accepted, a temporary, fourteen-day restraining order went into effect and a hearing date would be set to determine if the restraining order would continue.

I sat and waited, still wondering if I was doing the right thing. I had told Mitch many times that I would file. Until now, I never had. And therefore, he thought I never would. Was it fair to spring it on him? I told him it was over. I had gone no contact and stuck with it for months. This is the only way, I told myself. My propensity to be nice had gotten in the way of my own peace. Mitch's behavior would be the cause of his own embarrassment.

The clerk returned. "The judge needs to disqualify himself, but the fourteen-day order is granted," she said, and then pointed to the papers. "This is your hearing date and you'll be assigned an out-of-county judge."

Numbly, I walked down the courthouse stairs and along a hallway leading to the connecting sheriff's department. The lady behind the counter seemed like the designated neighborhood grandma from a time when kids freely roamed. Her warmth cracked my drone-like demeanor. I teared up a bit while filling out the paperwork to have Mitch served by a deputy.

"Sometimes you just gotta play hardball with certain folks," she said with an understanding nod. "A deputy will call you after he's been served."

Two-hundred and forty dollars later, I left the courthouse. The cost for a harassment restraining order could definitely be a barrier for some people. Then what? They'd have to put up with stalking bullshit from an ex-partner? That didn't seem fair. I felt fortunate I could cover the steep filing and sheriff's department fees.

About an hour after leaving the sheriff's department, a deputy called to let me know that Mitch had been served at his home. There was nothing to do but wait for the hearing.

Except there would never be a hearing.

28

Never again will my soul be for lease.

The day after filing, an email from Mitch arrived in my spam folder. Are you fucking kidding me? He broke the temporary order? His tone was all business.

Yolanda, In hopes of resolving your petition without a hearing, I've drafted the enclosed documents...

He asked me to sign documents that would avoid a hearing and stated that he would agree to a stipulation for a twelve-month no-contact order. Avoiding a hearing would certainly be less stressful.

How would I know the documents are real and that you won't throw them away after I sign? I wrote.

He said they would be filed and uploaded to our case on the court website...that he had access to seeing. He would send me screenshots of everything.

I'll sign if you reimburse me the $240 I spent to file, I wrote. He agreed. We met at a nearby school parking lot and I signed.

"I drafted and printed an affidavit form for you, stating that if you believe I have violated the no-contact agreement, you can take this to the courthouse and file it with the clerk," Mitch said all business-like.

Our meeting was quick and to the point. He ended with a tearful, "I love you." His tears didn't move me. I had learned that people like Mitch faked emotions to manipulate others. I didn't hate him. I just wanted to move on. I walked away, thinking we had signed a type of restraining order in lieu of a hearing. Mitch later sent me a screenshot of the uploaded order electronically signed by an out-of-county judge.

A few words come to mind.

Naive.

Credulous.

Gullible.

The year I spent on the trail only broke my addiction to Mitch and helped me understand that I had been in an abusive relationship. There was still a lot of work ahead of me to do to unravel the history and thought processes that drew me into that situation.

* * *

A few weeks later in mid-July, I spied an envelope from Mitch in my stack of mail. Unbelievable, I thought, shaking my head. Would this ever end? I lifted the completely flat envelope. Was it empty? I carefully opened it and spied a Post-it note filled with tiny writing on both sides. An entire letter's worth of words crammed onto both sides of the 3x3 inch piece of paper. The "letter" started out with…*Yolanda, please don't take this note as harassment*…and then went into a bizarre mish-mash of topics…a previous partner…his reasoning for using the term "effing cunt"…his hair and how he had never dyed it…a hike he took…how withholding intimacy was an effective behavior modification tool…and then ended with…*Thank you for hopefully understanding why I felt compelled to share this with you. I don't want an injunction against me. Mitch.* Two-hundred and eighteen words on a Post-it note.

So contacting me on a Post-it note didn't count? 'Cause it's so small? Like I'd let it slide because it's tiny?

He was testing me.

If a 3x3-inch paper ended up being okay, then next time it would be a card. Then endless email. More gifts. And another year of bullshit would go by. I wasn't surprised or shocked. That was Mitch. I took the note and the affidavit to the court house.

"I was told to bring this in if someone has violated a restraining order," I said to the same down-to-business clerk behind the window.

She took the paper from me and looked a bit perplexed.

"He broke a restraining order?" she asked in surprise.

"Yeah, he sent me this." I handed her the Post-it note. Her face softened. She took the note along with the affidavit.

"Wait just a moment and I'll upload this to your case," she said and disappeared around some file cabinets and desks. After returning to the window she seemed a bit unsure of what to tell me to do next. "Ummm…take these to the police department," she said, and slipped the papers back to me under the window.

* * *

I sat down with two officers in a little room at the police department.

"You're the victim of a crime here," one of them said. That was odd to hear. I didn't feel like the victim of a crime.

"We're going to get you in touch with our victim's advocate officer and we're going to see Mitch. We'll give you a call once we've visited."

Later that afternoon, a female victim's advocate called. She introduced herself as Officer Sarah. Her friendly and warm voice put me at ease. She didn't ask why I stayed in

SQUATTER

the relationship so long. She didn't ask why I hadn't seen the red flags. For the first time, someone wasn't putting it back on me. She simply held Mitch accountable for his behavior.

"If you agree, I'd like Amy at the Women's Community to get in touch with you," she said near the end of our conversation.

"I don't know if I really need that."

"They have resources that can help you with this situation."

I agreed and thanked Officer Sarah for her time.

Amy from the Women's Community called shortly afterwards, took some information and said she'd get back in touch with me.

I busied myself doing yard work. My phone buzzed in my pocket. The officer had visited Mitch. He sounded a bit ruffled. I wasn't surprised. Talking with Mitch exhausted the mind. He had a way of discombobulating people.

"What is it that you believe you signed, Yolanda?" he asked.

"A restraining order...that we agreed to out of court," I said, and closed my eyes in disbelief because I knew I was about to feel like an idiot.

"It wasn't a restraining order. It was a civil agreement... which basically means nothing," the officer said. "He knew there would be no consequences for contacting you."

"Oh my gosh, I feel so stupid. That was totally my own fault...I should have known what I was signing," I stammered.

"Don't feel stupid at all. People like Mitch are very skilled manipulators. He seemed like he was expecting us," the officer said. "I'm going to document the heck out of this."

I thought it was an odd thing for him to say. But then again, he dealt with Mitch, who left people with a weird what-the-hell-just-happened feeling. "We did issue him a stalking warning letter," he went on. "Stalking is a felony, so we made it clear to him that if he continues this behavior he could be charged with a felony." He also told me something that I didn't know, that breaking a restraining order was only a misdemeanor. I felt good about the stalking warning letter.

Amy from the Women's Community called back. I felt lighter and relieved at the support being offered. I didn't have to handle everything alone anymore.

"Did you know that this isn't the first time Mitch has gotten someone to back out of a restraining order filed against him?" Amy asked. "He's smart. Very smart. I have never encountered anything like this before."

"What?" My stomach twisted. Was she about to tell me that Mitch had been living some kind of double life all the time I had known him?

"I can tell you this because it's public record. Just a few months ago, someone else filed a restraining order against him in another county. He also convinced them to sign a civil agreement as well."

"Who?" I said. My pulse bounded, and I held my breath. She told me the name.

"Oh my god! That's his sister! I've met her!" I sat breathless and wide-eyed. That explained one of his recent, odd emails stating that he was looking for a new family.

Yeah. Looking for a new family to destroy.

"The Women's Community will provide you with an attorney if you decide to pursue a restraining order, but I'll tell you, it won't be easy. You will face him in court. If you don't have a lawyer, you will have to cross-examine him yourself."

Holy shit.

SQUATTER

"I had no idea that's how it would work," I said. I would have walked into a disaster if we had gone through with the hearing. I envisioned that we'd stand in front of the judge, I'd explain my reasons for wanting the order and that would be it. I decided not to pursue the restraining order now that Mitch had gotten the stalking warning letter.

"I'll also let you know that everything Mitch sees on the court site," she said, "You have access to as well."

I had been totally played. Actually, I had been played since day one. Maybe that was the real reason I laid on my bed and bawled after our first date. At the time, I'd thought my emotions ran high because moving on and pursuing change was a big step. But maybe…just maybe…my gut had sensed something about Mitch that was overwhelming. Maybe something about him had been subconsciously familiar to me and my spirit had warned me to stay away.

My time on the trail gave me the chance I needed to learn about myself. I came to understand that resilience, independence, and resourcefulness were my strengths. But I also came to see that I could be too trusting. More layers needed to be peeled back to get to the core of what had allowed me to tolerate Mitch's behavior. For that, I would need more time.

* * *

Months later, while rearranging furniture, something on the back of my bed's headboard caught my attention. Writing… words carved into the wood. I had purchased the oak frame from a thrift store many years ago. A beautiful find. How did I miss that? I shined my phone's flashlight on the scratching that spanned the whole length of the headboard.

Are you kidding me? I shook my head. Really, I wasn't surprised. During one of my many breakup attempts, Mitch had etched into the wood:

Yolanda DeLoach

Mitch + Yolanda
The sacrifice was nowhere to be found within her spirit.

How right he was. I may have lost myself for a time during those soul-crushing years, but I did not completely sacrifice my spirit. The human spirit is resilient. Even when reduced to smoldering ash, the spirit is able to spark back to life with the right conditions. I found those conditions in nature's touch and the hearts of others along Wisconsin's Ice Age Trail.

* * *

We are all on our own journey of self-discovery. There is no set timeline to follow or race to be won. Exposing the truths of our lives often includes removing many layers. Those layers can be as stubborn to remove as ancient wallpaper cemented to plaster walls. Sometimes it takes being in an abusive, toxic relationship before the toughest layer will release. It's often after such a relationship that one begins to connect the dots. To reexamine childhood experiences with new eyes. To see how early childhood attachment issues mar adult, intimate relationships.

I don't say this to assign blame. I say it to better understand and appreciate my journey. I was well into my fifties and the writing of this book when I had the epiphany I needed most: there isn't anything wrong with me.

Peace and Love,

Squatter

Acknowledgments

This story was brought to life with the influence and work of many people. Great appreciation and thanks to Dr. Ross Tangedal and the Cornerstone Press team for making this project a reality. A special thank you to my editor, Brett Hill, who shares my love of hiking. Thanks, also, to Carolyn Czerwinski for the cover design, and to Ava Willett, Natalie Reiter, and Sophie McPherson in media and sales.

Much thanks to my beta readers: Lee Augustine, Jennifer Baldock, Janice Peterson Hincapie, David Kelly, and Gail Lussenhop Pierce, who took the time to read the early, messy manuscript. Thank you Lisa Goetzinger and Amy Lagueux for reading the polished version.

To my writing group at Red Oak Writing, thank you for your honest feedback.

Thank you to Patty Dreier, Ed Abell, and Melanie Radzicki McManus for providing their kind words to encourage others to give this story a read.

All the thanks in the world isn't enough to give the workers and volunteers at the Ice Age Trail Alliance. Their work offers a sanctuary where life changing healing can occur.

Thank you to every person whose life touched mine during my time on the Ice Age Trail.

And to my kids and their families, thank you for being my people.

Yolanda DeLoach is an avid section hiker and outdoors advocate, having become a "1,000-miler" on the Ice Age Trail in 2021. She lives in Central Wisconsin, where she works as a palliative care/hospice registered nurse.

Printed in the USA
CPSIA information can be obtained
at www.ICGtesting.com
LVHW050309230124
769680LV00041B/878